W9-DBN-879

RAVES FROM THE NATION'S BEAUTY EDITORS FOR NICOLE RONSARD AND HER METHOD

VOGUE SAYS:

"If you ask Nicole Ronsard about cellulite, she could write a book. And she has. *The very first of its kind,* it's devoted exclusively to cellulite—a subject Mme. Ronsard has been studying all her life."

HARPER'S BAZAAR SAYS:

"Cellulite, in America, is still something of a mystery, but in Europe it has been recognized and treated for years. And it has been successfully controlled! Nicole Ronsard, an international authority on the cellulite problem . . . offers a way out from the fatty condition that has been (afflicting) millions of women."

THE NEW YORK TIMES SAYS:

"A Way to Correct Fat Gone Wrong. Mme. Ronsard describes cellulite as those unattractive areas of dimpled, rippling flesh resembling orange peel that seem to have little to do with a woman's age or weight."

COSMOPOLITAN SAYS:

"Spot reducing . . . used by Manhattan's Nicole Ronsard is gaining adherents . . . to break up the cellulite—those doughy patches of dimpled flab that congregate around buttocks, hips and thighs."

WOMEN'S WEAR DAILY SAYS:

"Fat-Gone-Wrong: Those lumps or bulges that look like fat but don't go away after dieting can be cellulite, pockets of fat and water that harden and form gel-like lumps in the layer of tissue between muscle and skin. *And Nicole Ronsard can tell you all the rules of fighting cellulite.*"

MADAME RONSARD SAYS:

"Almost every woman has—at one time or another—
a cellulite condition. It is our goal to help her
recognize it . . . and learn how to correct and
control it. Indeed, those lumps *can* be controlled.
My book shows the way through a sensible
'six-point' program especially designed
to help eliminate cellulite."

WHO IS NICOLE RONSARD?

European-trained, Nicole Ronsard has spent her years in America
leading the fight against cellulite. Her delightful New York salon
became a gathering place for figure-conscious women. Now, she
has adapted her proven salon method for women everywhere.
She has written a book that has become a phenomenal success,
that sold 500,000 copies in hardcover at the original price of
$12.95. *This is the original book.* Now you can do something
about cellulite.

There is no longer any reason to live with your lumps.

Cellulite:
Those lumps, bumps and bulges you couldn't lose before

by Nicole Ronsard

BANTAM BOOKS
TORONTO · NEW YORK · LONDON · SYDNEY

CELLULITE

A Bantam Book / published by arrangement with
Beauty & Health Publishing Corp.

PRINTING HISTORY

Beauty & Health edition published February 1973
24 printings through September 1974

Excerpts appeared in Redbook Beauty Book

Bantam edition / January 1975

2nd printing ..... January 1975	7th printing .... February 1975
3rd printing ..... January 1975	8th printing .... February 1975
4th printing .... February 1975	9th printing ...... March 1975
5th printing .... February 1975	10th printing .... March 1975
6th printing .... February 1975	11th printing .... April 1975
	12th printing ... April 1975

New Bantam edition / July 1975

2nd printing ... December 1975	9th printing .... November 1978
3rd printing ...... March 1976	10th printing... September 1979
4th printing .... April 1976	11th printing .... June 1980
5th printing ...... August 1976	12th printing .... July 1980
6th printing .... December 1976	13th printing ... November 1980
7th printing .... August 1977	14th printing ... December 1980
8th printing .... June 1978	15th printing... September 1981

Copyright © 1973 by Beauty & Health Publishing Corp.
All rights reserved.
This book may not be reproduced in whole or in part, by
mimeograph or any other means, without permission.
For information address: Beauty & Health Publishing Corp.
987 Lexington Avenue, New York, N.Y. 10021

ISBN   0-553-20705-9

Published simultaneously in the United States and Canada

Bantam Books are published by Bantam Books, Inc. Its trademark,
consisting of the words "Bantam Books" and the portrayal of a
rooster, is Registered in U.S. Patent and Trademark Office and in
other countries. Marca Registrada. Bantam Books, Inc., 666 Fifth
Avenue, New York, New York 10103.

PRINTED IN THE UNITED STATES OF AMERICA

24   23   22   21   20   19   18   17

ACKNOWLEDGMENTS

Many thanks to the following people:

Mary Butler
Jonas Ettlinger
Joan P. Goodman
Joe Haber
Nancy Horch
Phyllis Melhado
Lois Perlman

To my son

To my son

CONTENTS

THE CELLULITE STORY

If you ask Nicole Ronsard about cellulite, she could write a book. And she has—*Cellulite: Those Lumps, Bumps, and Bulges You Couldn't Lose Before.* The very first of its kind, it's devoted exclusively to cellulite—a subject Mme. Ronsard has been studying all her life. What prompted this putting-everything-down-in-black-and-white were the results she's been able to achieve in her New York treatment salon and the general lack of awareness concerning cellulite in this country. For the unenlightened, Mme. Ronsard defines cellulite as gel-like lumps composed of fat, water, and the residues of toxic substances that should be —but have not been—eliminated by the body. Lodged just below the surface of the skin—and most likely to lodge in the thighs—these lumps persist despite normal diet-and-exercise routines. Early on, we learn the causes of cellulite, how it can be recognized, and other places it usually affects. Then Mme. Ronsard gets down to the serious business of moving those immovable objects. Her plan of action is a six-point one: the proper diet; increasing the body's elimination; correct breathing; exercise geared to the trouble spots; massage; relaxation. All of which is clearly explained and illustrated both with photographs and attractive line drawings. Some of the things she touches upon—nutrition, deep breathing, swimming pool exercises, Yoga postures, ways to take it easy—make for an interesting, useful read—cellulite or no cellulite. . . .

Reprinted from the editorial pages of **Vogue**

PREFACE

Cellulite is practically a household word in Europe. It describes those lumps, bumps and bulges that won't go away with simple diet and exercise.

When I first arrived in the United States from France, I was amazed to find that so few people had even heard of cellulite, yet they were struggling so hard to fight it, without success. Americans have only lately begun to realize that cellulite is a special problem requiring very special corrective measures.

Once I began to treat cellulite, and word got around, letters started to pour in from all over America. Letters from women telling me all the ways they had tried, unsuccessfully, to lose those bulges that persist in ruining their figures and their self-confidence. Letters that describe the desperation they feel because they cannot wear the clothes they like, especially pants. Letters that tell of unhappiness and embarrassment because these women cannot walk down a beach, onto a tennis court or in front of a husband or lover without feeling ugly or unattractive. Letters from women begging for help.

This book was written in the hope that by identifying and understanding what causes your problem, you will be able to correct it. I have tried to keep the explanations simple, direct and easy to understand. There are many factors contributing to cellulite. All are discussed in depth.

However, before beginning any program of self-improvement, whether it be diet or exercise, it is always a good idea to check with your doctor on your general physical health. Then you can adapt the program to your personal requirements.

I have seen so many women come out of their depression once they solved their cellulite problems. Clothes fit right. Bathing suits are no longer embarrassing. Self-confidence builds up. The world starts looking rosy again. It is my most sincere wish that you, too, will find success in your struggle against cellulite.

NICOLE RONSARD

❧1❧

Plain Talk About Cellulite

If you have fat that just won't go away—no matter how much you diet or exercise—chances are it isn't just ordinary fat. You probably have cellulite*—one of the most common, unattractive and annoying figure problems. It's so common, in fact, that about eight out of ten women of all weights and ages are noticeably marred by the unattractive, dimpled, rippling masses of flab that characterize cellulite.

You've most likely seen cellulite hundreds of times thinking you were looking at simple, ordinary flab. You know, those "jodhpur thighs" or "saddlebag buttocks" that sort of sit on the sides of the upper thighs . . . or bumpy-looking legs with a texture that reminds you of cottage cheese . . . or knees that seem to be full of little lumps. Ring a bell? Well, all these figure distortions are caused by cellulite, not fat.

*pronounced *cell-u-leet*

How did cellulite get its name?

In Europe, women have been benefiting from cellulite treatments for years. They pay particular attention to the deposits on the upper thigh area which they call *culottes de cheval*. Literally translated from the French, this means riding breeches. Although the French are often credited with the discovery of cellulite, the distinction actually belongs to the Swedes. Toward the end of the nineteenth century, prominent Swedish doctors, masseurs and gymnasts understood the connection between body appearance and body health. So they developed a regimen of total body care that stressed a program of massage, exercise and proper diet. In their research, they discovered the presence of lumpy node-like formations just under the skin which they treated with a special method of massage, diet and exercise. Among the various names they gave these lumpy masses were Cellulite, Panniculite and Myocellulite. Always eager to maintain their leadership in the field of beauty, the French quickly adopted the name Cellulite and popularized it around the world.

Through years of usage in Europe, particularly France, the word cellulite has become synonymous with the "lumps and bulges" condition. However, confusion sets in because cellulite is also medically used in connection with cellulitis which dictionaries define as an inflammation of connective tissue. Cellulitis has no relationship with cellulite, the subject of this book.

Exactly what is cellulite?

Cellulite is the "fat" you just can't seem to lose. While normal fat can be lost with the usual regimen of diet or exercise, cellulite cannot—because it is more than simple fat. It is a gel-like substance made up of fat, water and wastes, trapped in lumpy, immovable pockets just beneath the skin. These pockets of "fat-gone-wrong" act like sponges that can absorb amounts of water, blow up and bulge out, resulting in the ripples and flabbiness you see.

Because cellulite is *not* regular fat, even the stingiest diet fails. When the normal intake of food is cut down, the body automatically burns its own reservoir of stored fat. On a low-calorie diet, fat will come off in many areas, but the cellulite bulges will remain. They do not burn up like normal fat. The cellulite diet is one that purifies the body of excess water and toxic wastes without forcing it to burn fat in unnecessary areas. This diet avoids those foods that tax an already over-burdened system, as they contribute to cellulite formation.

Specific areas are subject to cellulite

While regular fat can be found anywhere on the body, cellulite seems to "prefer" the following areas:

Inner, upper and back parts of the thighs

Inside the knees

Stomach

Hips

Buttocks

Lower back

Inside and back of upper arms

Ankles

Upper back, just below the shoulder blades

Why cellulite settles in these areas is still the subject of great controversy among experts. Although cellulite may be particular about *where* it strikes, it is not particular about *whom* it strikes. Women of all shapes and sizes, of all weights and ages are vulnerable. Cellulite has no prejudice!

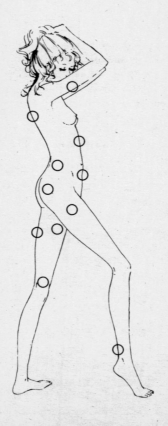

How to recognize cellulite

Now you know cellulite is different from regular fat. You know it is always found in the same areas. But how do you recognize it?

Visually, fat and cellulite are very different. Regular fat, when squeezed, is smooth in texture. In appearance it does not show any ripples or lumps.

To discover if you have a cellulite problem, there is one simple test that cannot fail. Here's how to do it:

Press (or squeeze) the tissues between the thumb and index finger or between the palms of both hands. If cellulite is present, the skin ripples and looks like a orange peel. There is also a characteristic sensitivity, not present when you squeeze a non-cellulite or simple fat area.

At a more advanced stage, the ripples will be noticeable without applying any pressure. Tissues will be flabby, and sensitivity no longer present in most cases.

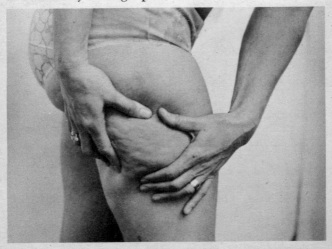

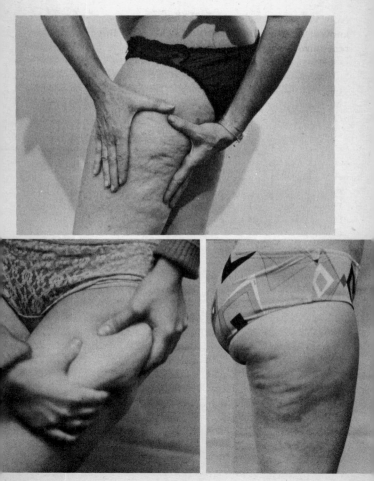

How is cellulite formed?

Your body is one of the most beautiful and functional machines ever designed! It is skin and bones, nerves and muscles, brain and blood supply all working together. Each part has a definite function in the whole scheme of living. We are interested here in one aspect of the scheme—the connective tissue.

All the muscles of the body are wrapped in a padding of fatty, connective tissue. This padding, with its varying thickness, gives the female figure its roundness and soft contour. The round fatty cells of the padding, bathed in a liquid medium, are held in place by a network of fibers. Constantly circulating through these are the nourishing liquids—water, blood and lymphatic fluid. These liquids carry oxygen and nutrients through the tissues and also cleanse them of wastes. The free flow of the liquids assures this process.

A change occurs when the waste removal process is slowed down in cellulite-prone areas. As a result, the connective tissue—saturated with water and wastes—thickens, hardens and forms immovable pockets. These bulge and puff up to produce the "orange peel" texture characteristic of cellulite.

Causes of cellulite

The way we live is really the ultimate cause of cellulite. Some of the contributing factors are:

> Tension
>
> Fatigue
>
> Poor eating habits
>
> Insufficient water intake
>
> Poor breathing
>
> Sedentary living
>
> Lack of proper exercise
>
> Polluted air

Results:

> Sluggish digestion
>
> Constipation
>
> Poor circulation

When these occur, the normal process of elimination cannot flush out toxic materials. Another contributing factor is estrogen. This female hormone is heavily secreted through the system a few days before each menstrual period and sometimes at the time of ovulation. At both times, the body generally retains water, accentuating the already bloated areas where cellulite is present.

Autointoxication

You can also think of cellulite as a kind of "poisoning" of the connective tissue. Our bodies have a marvelous system for eliminating wastes through the lungs, liver, kidneys, intestines and skin. But when we abuse our bodies, the normal processes of elimination are unable to completely flush out wastes and toxic materials. Common "poisons" can be everyday goodies that are all right in moderation but devastating in excess . . . alcohol . . . tea . . . coffee . . . spices . . . pork . . . animal fat . . . chocolate . . . cream . . . fried foods. These are the demons.

Too many pills and medications, taken without absolute necessity, are also to blame. Sleeping pills, diet pills and pep pills are examples. Cigarette smoking is another consideration in the fight against cellulite. It should be avoided, or at least cut down as much as possible. Think about your own habits and ask yourself if you are literally "poisoning" you body!

At what age does cellulite appear?

Cellulite can appear at any age, starting as early as 14 or 15 years. When this happens, it generally accompanies the onset of the menstrual cycle. Or it can make its first appearance much later in life, around the menopause. Cellulite can "happen" at any age.

Is cellulite hereditary?

While you don't actually inherit cellulite, the *tendency* to have cellulite may be hereditary. What you may acquire from parents is a certain style of living, with its diet, exercise and tension/stress patterns intact. If the diet is poor, exercise lacking, tension and stress constant, you'll probably have cellulite, because these are the cellulite-causing factors. But there's no need to accept bulging thighs or knees just because your mother has them! Something can and should be done about them. This book will teach you what and how.

Under what conditions does cellulite appear?

Cellulite is generally insidious, coming on slowly after the body has been abused for some time by such habits as poor eating, lack of proper exercise, too much alcohol and tobacco and so on, as we've already told you. But it can also happen quite suddenly, after an emotional shock, an accident, a long sickness or a drastic change in one's life.

Among many women it is birth control pills or pregnancy that seem to bring it on. Why? Because during pregnancy, the system is flooded with the estrogen hormone that favors water retention and results in bloating. Also, the unusual stress on the body interferes with proper blood circulation in the veins and often causes constipation. These conditions are sometimes conducive to the formation of cellulite.

As for birth control pills, they technically simulate pregnancy. A high estrogen content is a responsible factor in retaining water in the tissues and may interfere with proper circulation in the veins.

Why is cellulite a feminine problem?

While men will sometimes find cellulite on the stomach and at the nape of the neck, it is largely a feminine problem for several reasons. Women have more than twice as much fatty tissue as men. (In general, normal fat represents 24% of a woman's weight and only 11% of a man's.) So women have more to "work with" in forming the lumpy combination of water, fat and wastes. Also, the female hormone, estrogen, seems to create a setting conducive to cellulite formation.

A woman's physical makeup and her emotions are often closely linked. When her emotions and nerves get caught up in tension and anxiety, she is prone to cellulite.

To summarize, cellulite is formed in the connective tissue by:

1. Slowing down of the waste removal process.
2. Hardening of the connective tissue.
3. Imprisonment of wastes.

So, in order to correct a cellulite condition, these three steps must be reversed by:

1. Returning the connective tissue to its normal elasticity and suppleness.
2. Freeing the trapped substances.
3. Draining and removing these materials.

It must be stressed that these three steps are interdependent. Each must be given individual attention and all three must be carefully followed to effectively alleviate a cellulite condition. These are precisely what you will learn to do as you continue reading this book.

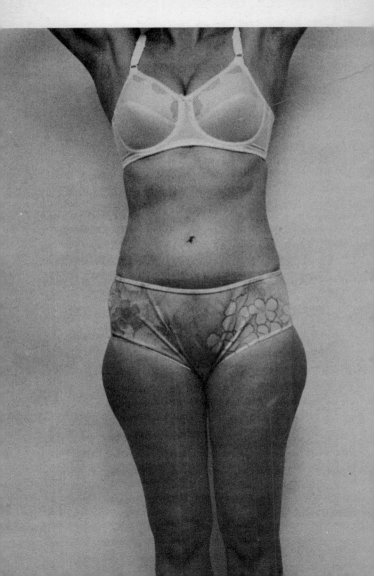

❧2❧

What Does Cellulite Look Like?

Cellulite masses make the parts of the body on which they form very heavy and out of proportion. Sometimes the masses themselves are so distorted they look like they do not even belong to the body.

There are two basic types of cellulite—solid and soft. The form it eventually takes depends upon its "breeding ground."

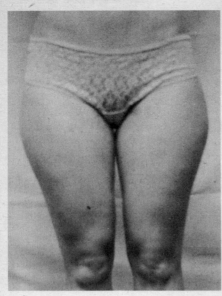

Cellulite of the upper thigh in the early stage, the beginning of the common "slack problem."

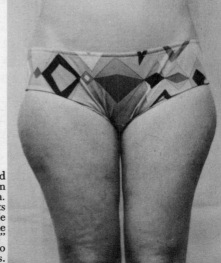

More advanced case of cellulite on the upper thigh. This picture depicts clearly the "culotte de cheval" or the "riding breeches" that ruin so many good figures.

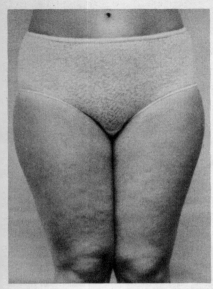

This is a good example of solid cellulite affecting both the thigh and the knee.

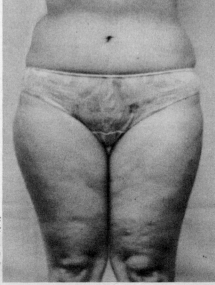

Advanced case of soft cellulite of the entire thigh and knee area showing the lumpy, "cottage cheese" texture.

How can you recognize solid cellulite?

Sometimes it is difficult to visually recognize solid or firm cellulite right away. This thick cellulite tissue seems to stick to the muscles. You can hardly lift the cellulite away from its underlying structure. And if you squeeze or press the tissues you'll notice they are sensitive to the touch. This is because some nerve endings have probably become compressed.

On whom is solid cellulite found?

While there are exceptions, solid cellulite is generally found on young women in good physical condition. But women of all ages are vulnerable including those with firm, well-toned tissues—athletic types, you might say. (It is very common among dancers, for example.) These are women who have probably never experienced extreme weight variations or followed crash diets, both extremely destructive measures. Since their tissues have not been mistreated, they remain firm.

What problems accompany solid cellulite?

The skin in cellulite areas is generally dry—sometimes rough, due to poor nourishment. Stretch marks are another problem. Flexible, elastic fibers enable skin to move, stretch and contract. However, when these fibers are stretched too much, or for too long a period of time, they rupture, leaving scar-like traces. These stretch marks often occur after pregnancy. The same is true when they appear as a result of cellulite because the skin cannot cope with the excess underneath.

How can you recognize soft cellulite?

Here the picture changes quite a bit. Soft cellulite is neither compact nor concentrated like solid cellulite. Instead, it tends to occupy large areas, is loose and seems to *float* between muscles and skin. This kind of cellulite is quite noticeable and has made life miserable for countless women.

It is hardly necessary to feel the tissues to recognize this kind of cellulite. Unlike the firm variety, soft cellulite has great mobility, sliding easily over the muscle. Because it is loose, it hangs and sags in folds and flabby bulges. It shakes with every bodily movement-hardly an attractive sight!

Who would most likely have soft cellulite?

Soft cellulite is often found on once active women who have been inactive for quite awhile. Some others have the physical makeup that can result in soft cellulite. Their tissues lack firmness. Skin is soft. Muscle tone is poor or nonexistent. Veins dilate easily.

There is another contributing factor: *crash dieting*. This kind of eating, with its quick, severe deprivation, is terribly abusive to the body. And even though most women on the up-again, down-again syndrome lose weight quickly, they gain it back just as fast. Tissues lose their elasticity and firmness with this fat-again, thin-again type of treatment, becoming soft and saggy.

Still another explanation indicts diuretic pills on which many women depend to lose weight quickly. It may seem fantastic to lose up to five pounds in a single day, but this is only water; and the weight returns as soon as the pills are stopped. Some women tend to use these pills too frequently, and, as with crash dieting, these weight and volume variations eventually deteriorate the tissues.

Both crash dieting and water loss through pills are extremely detrimental to women with cellulite. The way to lose weight, and keep it off, is to lose gradually with a well-rounded diet. Diuretics (water pills) should be taken only when really necessary and always under the supervision of a doctor. (In a later chapter you'll learn how to eliminate excess fluids naturally, without upsetting your system in any way.)

Cellulite and circulation problems

Circulation problems and cellulite seem to go hand-in-hand. Cellulite generally "chooses" areas that have poor circulation to begin with and, once it forms, cellulite slows circulation even more. When this happens to the legs, they often feel heavy and tired, especially at the end of the day.

Sitting down for long periods of time creates a sort of circulation "blockage" in the whole lower part of the body. Frequent crossing of the legs and wearing tight, restrictive underwear—girdles especially—all aggravate poor circulation.

People with cellulite frequently find themselves with unattractive broken blood vessels and troublesome varicose veins. And bruises are often a problem. The slightest hit can produce a discoloration.

❊3❊

What You Can Do About Those Lumps, Bumps And Bulges

Cellulite can be successfully treated. Indeed, very fine results have been achieved with a program of diet, breathing and oxygenation, exercise, proper elimination, massage and relaxation. Thousands of women have been able to change their figures significantly.

Fortunately, the measures used to treat cellulite are relatively simple. But they must be used *together*. Followed individually, they stop short of being really effective. Combined in a comprehensive *six-point program*, however, they can achieve gratifying results.

1. *Diet*

The first step is to follow a healthful and purifying diet. While the main objective of an ordinary reducing diet is the avoidance of high-calorie foods, a cellulite diet eliminates foods that leave toxic residues in the body.

2. *Proper Elimination*

The body primarily cleanses itself of waste materials through the kidneys, intestines and skin. Cleansing can be stimulated by increasing the volume of urine, by avoiding constipation and by activating perspiration. When these three organs "work overtime," the breakdown of cellulite is speeded up.

3. *Breathing and Oxygenation*

Deep breathing is an excellent way to help "burn up" cellulite-causing wastes left in the connective tissue. Because it brings great amounts of oxygen into the body, deep breathing helps to purify the blood and rid the system of toxic residues.

4. *Exercise*

The benefits of exercise are many. It stimulates circulation, breathing, digestion and elimination. It "revs up" metabolism. And it helps to replace cellulite with good muscle tone and firm tissues, while aiding in the relief of tension.

5. *Massage*

This reinforces the benefits of exercise. Massage can be done on specific cellulite bulges in individual areas to directly stimulate circulation where it is most needed. It is particularly helpful for those parts of the body that are difficult to reach with exercise, like the inside of the knee and the upper part of the thigh.

6. *Relaxation*

Relaxation is the antidote to stress and tension—definitely causes of cellulite. The aim is relaxation of the entire system, body *and* mind. When muscles are totally at ease, circulation is equalized and the release of toxic residues is encouraged, both tremendously important in the breakdown of cellulite.

These are steps that form the comprehensive, *six-point program.* When followed faithfully, these efforts will prove that you *can* do something to alleviate a distressing problem. Exactly *how* will be discussed in the following chapters.

·✣4✣·

The Right Way To Eat

Before getting into the specific cellulite control program, it is important that you know something about nutrition.

Knowing which foods *conribute* to cellulite and which help *control it* is essential. While this book is not meant to make you an expert in nutrition, it will show you that what you eat has a tremendous effect on your cellulite problems. *Keep in mind that your whole body·is inter-related.* If you neglect any aspect, your system goes out of kilter to a greater or lesser degree. Food plays a vital role in your good health, your good looks and in the way your figure ultimately shapes up.

Foods today are so over-processed and refined that they usually reach us robbed of most of their original, nutritional properties. Often they actually end up as empty foods. This is the case, for example, with white sugar and white flour products such as bread and cake. These foods have little nutritional value and offer nothing but starch and calories.

You will be doing your body a favor if you cultivate a taste for wholesome, natural foods that are also good for you. Choose fresh foods rather than canned, "convenience" varieties. *Learn to choose foods for their nutritional value rather than taste alone.* Once you learn the basics, you can prepare delicious meals that offer maximum nutrition. Make use of the many fine cookbooks available at health food stores and health food departments.

These are the ways your body uses up food:

Digestion is the process in which the food eaten is broken down into a form suitable for absorption by the body.

Assimilation converts digested food into nutritional material that can be delivered throughout the body.

Metabolism is a catch-all phrase referring to all the processes—digestion, assimilation plus circulation, respiration and excretion—involved in providing energy for the body. Generally speaking, it means the utilization of foods for the life of the muscles, nerves, tissues and cells.

As you know, the body needs certain substances in order to function. Here is a brief run-down on what these substances are and how they service the body.

Proteins

The basic building material which forms a major portion of all living tissue is protein. Without it there could be no life. The word "protein" itself actually means "primary."

Essentially made up of nitrogen, carbon, hydrogen and oxygen, proteins are broken down into amino acids during digestion, 22 of which are vital for life. Some are synthesized in the body. The rest—8 in number, called essential amino acids—must be supplied in adequate quantities through everyday diet.

If all 8 essential amino acids are present in the right proportions, a protein is *complete*. Most of the complete proteins are derived from animal sources: milk (fresh or powdered), yogurt, cheese, eggs, fish, fowl and meat. Soybeans, dried brewers' yeast, certain nuts and wheat germs are also complete proteins. Legumes, rice, flour and cereal lack the proper concentration of some of the essential amino acids and are called *incomplete* proteins.

Carbohydrates

While protein is the building and repairing substance of the body, carbohydrates and fats are its sources of energy, providing the fuel necessary to keep it going. Derived mainly from plant foods, carbohydrates are broken down, during digestion, into simple sugars—glucose, fructose and lactose. The most valuable carbohydrate foods supply the quick energy the body needs. Sources of high quality starches and sugars are whole-grain bread and cereals, brown rice, sweet fruits, vegetables and their delicious juices. Pure, natural honey, unsulphured molasses and dried fruits of all kinds are also excellent. "Empty" or useless calories are found in sugar, candy, soft drinks, potato chips, many of the cold cereals, pastries, etc. They have no use whatsoever and generally end up stored as unwanted fat.

Fats

Fats are actually concentrated energy-producing substances. When oxidized, they provide twice as much energy as carbohydrates and proteins. In addition, they must be present in order for Vitamins A, D, E and K to be absorbed by the blood. During the digestive process, fats are broken down into glycerin (glycerol) and fatty acids. Most of these fatty acids, derived primarily from sugar, can be manufactured by the body even when no fat is eaten. But three of them, called essential fatty acids, are absolutely necessary to the maintenance of health: linoleic, linolenic and arachidonic acids. These cannot be manufactured by the body and must be supplied through food. Pure, natural vegetable oils—safflower, soybean, sunflower, corn, wheat germ and cottonseed—are the best sources. Margarine, cream and butter supply little in the way of essential fatty acids. Because of its high Vitamin A content, however, a reasonable amount of butter is a very valuable part of any diet.

Vitamins

Vitamins act in many ways to regulate body processes. Vitamins help us burn and properly utilize foods. They are so important that even slight deficiencies prevent maximum health and well-being. Just the tiniest lack can result in fatigue, irritability and nervousness. Most vitamins are obtained from food. Others are actually produced in the body by the action of bacteria in the intestine.

Vitamin A

Derived from carotene, a yellow pigment found in many plants, Vitamin A is necessary for strong bones and teeth, good vision and firm, smooth skin. It can be found in carrots, beets, tomatoes, dark green leafy and deep yellow vegetables, fish liver oils, eggs, butter, milk and liver.

Vitamin B Complex

This important group is made up of different vitamins that are found together in various foods and work closely together as well. The B complex is sometimes called the "nerve vitamin" because it helps the nervous system function. It is also involved in the process of food burning, the formation of hemoglobin (red blood cells) and tissue activity. In addition, it helps to keep hair, skin and eyes healthy. Most of the vitamins of the B complex are found in dried brewers' yeast and wheat germ.

The individual vitamins that make up the B complex are: thiamine (B-1), riboflavin (B-2), pyridoxine (B-6), cyanocobalamin (B-12), niacin, folic acid, pantotenic acid, choline, inositol and biotin.

Thiamine (B-1)—Essential for good digestion, proper elimination, and healthy nerves, thiamine can be found in wheat germ, whole grains, liver, brewers' yeast, eggs, molasses, nuts and soy beans.

Riboflavin (B-2)—This compound helps tissues breathe and contributes to healthy skin, bright eyes and calm nerves. It is also a direct participant in the metabolism of proteins and carbohydrates. Milk, liver, cottage cheese, yogurt, brewers' yeast, avocados, leafy green vegetables, wheat germ, eggs and peas are all rich in riboflavin.

Pyridoxine (B-6)—Important in the utilization of proteins and fats, pyridoxine helps in the formation of blood as well as in the proper functioning of the muscles and nerves. Good sources are liver, wheat germ, brewers' yeast, whole grains, molasses, egg yolks, milk, nuts and green vegetables.

Cyanocobalamin (B-12)—found in organ meats (liver, kidneys, heart, brains), eggs, milk and fish, cyanocobalamin is indispensable in the formation of red blood cells.

Niacin—Required for the normal functioning of the liver and nervous system, niacin is also necessary in the oxidation of starches and sugars. It can be found in lean meat, organ and muscle meats such as liver, kidneys and heart, and in wheat germ, brewers' yeast, leafy green vegetables, powdered skim milk and fish.

Folic Acid—Essential for the formation of red blood cells, folic acid can be found in organ and glandular meats, brewers' yeast and leafy, green vegetables.

Pantothenic Acid—Needed for the healthy functioning of the digestive system, pantothenic acid participates in carbohydrate metabolism and also appears to increase resistance to mental stress. Sources are liver, kidneys, heart, brewers' yeast, egg yolk, soy beans, broccoli, mushrooms and peas.

Choline—Required for the proper utilization of cholesterol, choline affects the distribution of fat throughout the body, helping to prevent its accumulation in the liver. Choline can be found in egg yolks, liver, brewers' yeast, wheat germ, nuts and leafy green vegetables.

Inositol—This compound works closely with choline, both in distribution of fat and protection of the liver. It also fights against hardening of the arteries by preventing cholesterol from settling in them. In addition, it helps the body absorb Vitamin E. Found in liver, kidneys, brewers' yeast, wheat germ, fruit, whole grains and soy beans.

Biotin—Needed for the digestion and assimilation of fats, biotin is also necessary for good mental health. It can be found in brewers' yeast, wheat germ and liver.

Vitamin C

Often referred to as ascorbic acid, Vitamin C is important in the fight against infection. It is required for the formation and health of connective tissue and the strengthening of capillary walls. Consequently, it helps to prevent unsightly broken blood vessels and bruises. Vitamin C also helps to prevent fatigue. The richest natural source is rose hips, available in tablet form. It is also present in citrus fruits, tomatoes, red peppers and fresh, leafy green vegetables.

Vitamin D

Produced in the body when the skin is exposed to sunshine, Vitamin D is needed for strong bones and teeth. It is also important for the body's proper utilization of calcium and phosphorus. Rich sources are fish liver oil, milk and eggs.

Vitamin E

Able to store oxygen, Vitamin E is needed by the blood vessels and is essential for the proper functioning of the endocrine glands. It also participates in the breaking down of fats. Wheat germ, wheat germ oil, corn oil and peanut oil are all rich in Vitamin E.

Vitamin F

Another name for unsaturated fatty acids, Vitamin F is needed for the distribution of calcium and the absorption of fat soluble Vitamins A, D, E and K. Pure vegetable oils contain Vitamin F.

Vitamin K

This vitamin, manufactured by the body, plays an essential role in the clotting of the blood, thus helping to prevent hemorrhages. It is found in all green leafy vegetables, spinach, broccoli, cabbage, lettuce, etc.

Vitamin P

Required for strong, healthy capillaries, Vitamin P works together with Vitamin C and has the same sources: rose hips, citrus fruits, tomatoes, red peppers and fresh, leafy green vegetables.

Minerals

These important substances are present in the body in small but extremely vital amounts. Minerals are essential for a healthy nervous system and work in association with vitamins in the different metabolic processes. In addition, they regulate the water balance in the body.

Calcium

Essential to the maintenance of strong bones and teeth as well as the health and efficiency of the muscles, calcium also helps to promote good sleep and prevent irritability, nervous tension and muscles cramps. Sources of calcium are milk, powdered skim milk, Swiss, Parmesan and yellow cheeses, yogurt and molasses.

Phosphorus

Working in association with calcium, phosphorus participates in converting protein to amino acids as well as in the assimilation of fats and carbohydrates. In order for calcium and phosphorus to be assimilated by the body, however, Vitamin D must be present. Phosphorus is found in poultry, fish, meat, soy beans, cranberries and whole grains.

Iron

Iron is vital to the absorption of oxygen by the lungs, and its subsequent transportation to the cells. It also plays an important part in the oxidation of food nutrients and is a component of hemoglobin as well. While iron is important to everyone, women in particular need an extra supply. Sources rich in iron are liver, eggs, oysters, leafy green vegetables, legumes, nuts, skim milk, molasses, dried fruits, dried yeast, wheat germ.

Iodine

This mineral acts as a catalyst and is essential for the proper functioning of the thyroid—the gland directly related to control of body weight. Iodine is present in fish, shellfish and sea greens.

Sodium

Sodium is needed for the maintenance of body fluids. The excess amounts of sodium eaten by Americans as table salt has a direct bearing on bloating. (The daily requirement from all sources is just less than one tablespoonful.) Sodium occurs naturally in clams, oysters and white fish, wheat germ, brown rice, greens, celery, carrots, artichokes and molasses.

Potassium

Along with sodium, potassium also controls the body's water balance. It has a direct effect on the nervous system and is found in legumes (dried peas, beans, lentils, etc.), meat, fish, molasses, fresh fruits and vegetables, dried fruits, paprika, grape, apple and cranberry juices.

Magnesium

Important for relaxation of the body's muscles, magnesium also promotes elimination. Sources of magnesium are leafy greens, clams, nuts, whole grains and pure, natural honey.

Other important minerals present in the body and needed for its proper functioning are manganese, aluminum, sulphur, zinc, chlorine, copper, cobalt, fluorine, nickel and bromine.

A few rules to keep in mind when buying and preparing food for sound nutrition

Meats

Always buy meats as lean as possible and never eat the fat. Avoid serving gravies and rich sauces. Prepare meats in the most healthful way either by broiling or, for larger cuts, by roasting in a slow oven. This applies to poultry as well. From a nutritional point of view, organ meats such as liver, kidneys, and heart are the best.

Fish

Fish is an excellent alternative to meat. It is low in fat and is full of easily digested protein. Like meat, it should be broiled or baked in the oven. Fish tastes marvelous cooked with lemon juice and a variety of spices such as sage, thyme, etc.

Eggs

The best way to prepare eggs is by poaching or hard-boiling. If you want to scramble them, use pure vegetable oil rather than butter or another animal fat. However, the most healthful way of scrambling eggs is to use a teflon pan with no fat at all. Always cook eggs with low heat and be sure the pan is covered. This helps retain the vitamin content that is so easily destroyed by light. Try to buy organic or fertile eggs. They are well worth the additional cost.

Cheese

Always choose naturally processed cheeses and give preference to uncolored varieties since most yellow cheeses contain food coloring. To protect the vitamin content, keep cheese covered, wrapped in foil or waxed paper, and stored in a cool place.

Vegetables

Vegetables should be bought as fresh and crisp as possible and kept in a cool, dark place to safeguard their vitamin content. They should never be soaked but washed and scrubbed as thoroughly and as quickly as possible. Both peeling and over-cooking should be avoided. For maximum nutritional value, cook vegetables a short time in a heavy pot with a very small quantity of water. In this way, the liquid can be absorbed without loss of nutrients. If you use a lot of water, nearly all the vitamins and minerals are dissipated and generally discarded with the water! For the best results, bring about three tablespoons of water to a boil. Add the vegetables, sliced or cut in small pieces. Simmer, tightly covered, for just a few minutes.

Steaming vegetables in a pressure cooker or cooking in a special waterless utensil also preserves nutrients. Never add salt during cooking since this tends to draw out the minerals and much of the flavor. Instead, lightly salt the vegetables just before serving. Butter, if desired, also should be added at this time. Never discard whatever liquid remains after cooking. Serve it with the vegetables or save it for future use in soups and gravies. And never use soda when cooking vegetables. Although it may make them *look* greener, it destroys their vitamin content.

The time spent preparing fresh vegetables and fruits is a wonderfully healthful way to get closer to nature. And, if you are tempted to snack, you can just pop some raw slices of whatever you are preparing into your mouth.

Salads

In France and Italy, salads are included on all menus. Aside from being crisp and delicious, a salad provides an opportunity to eat vegetables raw, which delivers the most nutritional value. It's good to know that Americans, too, are eating more salads.

Vegetables used in a salad should never be soaked. Instead, wash them thoroughly in cold water and dry either with a towel or in a special wire basket designed for air-drying. Either way, drying is a must for delicious salads. It helps the dressing adhere, seals in the chlorophyl and keeps the salad fresh and crisp.

The best salad dressing is pure, natural vegetable oil with vinegar or lemon juice. In France, where a meal is not complete without a salad, the recipe for dressing is three parts oil to one part vinegar. Prepared, commercial dressings should be avoided. Aside from the fact that they are not as tasty as freshly prepared dressing, they are generally loaded with preservatives.

The secret of a delicious salad lies in the tossing. This should be done just before eating. Put the vegetables in a bowl, add the dressing (vinegar and oil lightly whipped together), and toss, gently picking up the ingredients between a fork and spoon—preferably wooden—lifting and mixing until each dry piece is coated. Add spices such as oregano, dill, basil, etc., and toss lightly once more. This tossing takes only a few seconds and it makes all the difference! Salad vegetables range beyond the lettuce family. Spinach, watercress, and endives can be substituted for, or added to lettuce. Other appetizing additions are carrots, bell peppers, raw beets, cauliflower and broccoli. A salad can be one of the most creative food preparations. While delicious, its leafy, green vegetables provide a greater concentration of vitamins and minerals than any other type of fresh food. If you don't have the time to prepare a salad, serve an appetizer of attractively displayed fresh, raw vegetables such as radishes, cucumbers, celery and carrots.

Fruits

Fresh fruits make ideal desserts and between-meal snacks. Because they are delicious as well as nutritional, they should be served frequently in salads and for appetizers as well. To retain the nutritive value of fruit, the same rules apply as those suggested for preparing salads and cooking vegetables. To protect their vitamin content, keep fresh fruits in the refrigerator or in a dark, cool place. They are apt to lose their vitamin content when left at room temperature. Exceptions to this rule are those fruits with heavy skin such as bananas and citrus varieties. Like vegetables, fruit should never be soaked, but washed quickly in cold water. Trim as little as possible and never peel or cut until shortly before serving to protect the Vitamin C content.

Choose fresh fruits rather than canned or frozen varieties. Because ripe, fresh fruits contain natural sugar, you don't really need any additional sweetener. If you must add sweetener, however, use a bit of pure honey rather than "empty" table sugar.

Vegetable juices

One of the easiest and tastiest ways to get loads of natural vitamins and minerals is to use a vegetable juice extractor. It's one of the best health and beauty "buys" you can make! You can use one vegetable at a time or combine two or more. The delicious possibilities are practically endless!

Never peel the vegetables when making juice. Simply scrub them with a vegetable brush under running, cold water. When you use the extractor, be sure that the juice flows into a porcelain, glass or stainless steel bowl. Tin or aluminum can affect the vitamin and mineral content of the juice, as well as the color and taste. Since the juices are very sensitive to air, you should drink them immediately after extraction, preferably sipped through a straw. If you must prepare juice for later use, be sure to refrigerate it in a tightly covered container and try to use it as soon as possible.

For maximum benefits, drink two glasses of fresh vegetable juice every day. Try celery, tomato, carrot or drink a whole salad! The great advantage of these juices is that you can easily drink as much as one pound of vegetables in a single glass. And you can use the juice extractor to make the most delicious fruit juices you have ever had! Virtually all the fruits are good—berries, peaches, apples, grapes, pineapples, etc.

Some "special" foods

Garlic—Among other things, garlic contains sulphur and iodine. It is a natural blood purifier and antiseptic. Garlic stimulates circulation, helps to prevent varicose veins and facilitates digestion to mention only a few of its "talents." Since cooking destroys most of its properties, garlic is best eaten raw. For those who do not get enough raw garlic in their daily diet, there are garlic tablets available, free from both odor and taste. You can help neutralize the odor of fresh, raw garlic by chewing some fresh parsley.

Powdered Skim Milk—Because it is high in protein, vitamins and minerals, and practically fat-free, powdered skim milk is a valuable concentrated food. Actually, it is the most inexpensive source of first-class protein. There are many good ways to use it to fortify a variety of dishes and drinks. For example, you can double the protein content of a quart of fresh milk, either skim or whole, by adding one cup of powdered skim milk. Powdered skim milk stays fresh stored in a tightly closed container in the refrigerator.

Yogurt—Rich in protein, B vitamins and calcium, yogurt is an excellent food that is particularly valuable in helping your intestinal tract stay healthy. It is ideal for dessert, snacks or meal substitutes when you are in a hurry. It even makes a delicious salad dressing. Plain yogurt is preferable to the flavored varieties which are full of preserves and white sugar. To sweeten plain yogurt add your own fresh fruit, pure honey or molasses.

Vegetables Oils—Pure, natural vegetable oils are extremely important to your health and good looks. Contrary to what most people think, they actually help burn up fat deposits and do not add weight. With the exception of fresh butter, they should be the only fats in your diet. Try to eat two tablespoonfuls every day. The best oils are sunflower, cottonseed, corn, peanut, soybean, wheat germ, sesame and olive. If possible, get the cold-pressed oils. They contain no additives of any kind. Always keep oils in a cool place.

Wheat Germ—The very heart and most nutritious part of the wheat, wheat germ is a rich source of protein, iron plus the B and E vitamins. It can easily be sprinkled on cereals, soups, salads and the like. It can also be incorporated in pancakes, waffles, breads, muffins and other baked goods. Mixed with sliced fruit and milk, it makes an ideal cereal itself. Wheat germ should always be refrigerated in a tightly covered jar.

Yeast—Brewers' yeast is a very valuable food. It contains complete proteins, many vitamins, especially the B vitamins, and various minerals, including all the essential trace minerals. But here's fair warning: brewers' yeast has a taste that many find difficult to get used to. *Persevere!* It's well worth the effort. Try the different brands available to find out which is most palatable. Brewers' yeast is far superior in nutritional value to yeast flakes and is much more concentrated than yeast tablets. For maximum benefits, stir one tablespoonful of brewers' yeast into a glass of milk, fruit or vegetable juice twice daily.

Honey—Pure honey is the ideal sweetening agent. Aside from being rich in minerals and Vitamins B and C, it is the best source of quick energy. As the simplest form of natural sugar, it is readily assimilated into the bloodstream. The ancient Egyptians, Greeks and Romans associated the bee with their gods and considered honey a gift from heaven. It takes a full 18 hours of strenuous labor for a bee to produce a single drop of honey. To produce a pound, the bee must put in an equivalent of 30-40,000 miles, going from hive to flower and back again. This represents one and a half times the circumference of the earth! When you think about it, you should really appreciate having this "living sugar." And when you buy honey, make sure the label specifies "guaranteed pure and natural."

·❧5❧·

The Diet That Gets After Cellulite

Cellulite is not ordinary fat. It cannot be lost through ordinary dieting. On a reducing diet, for example, a normal-weight person with cellulite bulges on the upper thighs will lose everywhere except on those thighs! And with the rest of the body thinned out, the bulges will be even more noticeable. Most cellulite, it seems, is not accompanied by overweight. But if overweight and cellulite are both problems, it is preferable to lose the extra weight before starting the anti-cellulite program. Although there are plenty of diets from which to choose, be sure to pick one that provides balanced eating rather than a fad, crash-type program. This will enable you to retain your eating habits so that once you get the excess weight off, you will be able to keep it off.

The anti-cellulite diet is designed to help rid the body of toxic waste. *Purification and elimination are its primary goals, not weight loss.* So it calls, not for calorie deprivation, but for foods that are bland and easy to digest, and those which help the body "burn" waste materials. Heavy, rich foods that tend to overload the liver and make digestion difficult are prohibited.

Know your liver

The stress on good digestion is the key to your anti-cellulite diet. It is important that you realize the liver plays a particularly vital role in the digestive process. It produces protein, processes iron for the blood system and detoxifies some of the poisons that enter the bloodstream. This last, anti-toxic function is especially crucial to the cellulite problem. When the liver is working properly, it easily neutralizes all toxic products which can then be eliminated through the kidneys and intestines. But when it is over-burdened, it loses its ability to *completely* neutralize all of the poisons that enter the bloodstream. Some of these poisons eventually will accumulate in the connective tissue and lay the groundwork for the formation of cellulite.

The Do-Gooders

The anti-cellulite diet is actually pleasant. It's also quite simple to follow! Read the following list of preferred foods and see why:

Vegetables—a substantial portion to be eaten raw

Fruit—also raw

Salads—with pure, natural, vegetable oil dressing

Vegetable juices—freshly extracted

Eggs—prepared without butter or fat

Cheese—low-fat varieties

Yogurt—without preserves (add your own fresh fruits instead)

Milk—preferably skim

Meat, poultry and fish—lean, prepared by broiling or roasting, and eaten in moderation

6 to 8 glasses of water—spaced throughout the day

Dried brewers' yeast—optional, but highly recommended (Two teaspoons stirred into some fruit or vegetable juice taken 15 minutes before meals. Yeast is a rich source of proteins and vitamins, especially Vitamin B, so important for good elimination. In addition, yeast is a good appetite depressant.)

As you can see, the mainstays of the anti-cellulite diet are actually fresh fruits and vegetables. Try to eat them at each meal. Meat, fish or poultry, on the other hand, should be eaten no more than once a day and preferably every other day. *Cut down on salt* as much as possible and avoid drinking liquids *with* meals.

What about bread and other starches?

If you happen to be thin, you can eat them in moderation. If you have a tendency to gain weight, you should avoid them by all means.

Look over this sample menu. The foods suggested are tasty and nutritious as well as beneficial to your cellulite program.

Try using this menu as a guide. But remember it is only a *guide*. There are many alternatives from which to choose. (See preceding page.)

SAMPLE MENU

BREAKFAST

Half a grapefruit or fresh fruit in season
1 or 2 poached eggs
Weak or decaffeinated coffee

MIDMORNING

(If hungry)
Fresh fruit or large glass of freshly
extracted vegetable juice

LUNCH

Crudités*—carrots, celery, cucumbers,
tomatoes, radishes, etc. Large salad bowl
(including cottage cheese if you like)
Yogurt

MIDAFTERNOON

(If hungry)
Fresh fruit or vegetable juice

DINNER

Crudités*
Broiled, lean fish or meat
Cooked, green vegetable
Leafy salad
Fresh fruit

*Crudités is French for raw vegetables.

A few words about salt

Salt is used entirely too much by most people and its over-use contributes significantly to cellulite. As you have already learned, the cellulite condition results partly from water trapped in the tissues. Salt is often to blame. It tends to retain fluids in the tissues. And women who develop cellulite are generally those who already have a tendency toward water-retention.

It's very important, therefore, that salt intake be restricted as much as possible to prevent further retention and to facilitate the release of the fluid already trapped. This means to avoid adding salt to food and, equally necessary, to avoid those foods containing great amounts of salt, such as the ones listed on page 68, plus flavorings such as celery salt, garlic salt and the like. Whenever possible, avoid canned and processed foods, as they contain enormous quantities of salt.

Do not be afraid of a sodium chloride (table salt) deficiency when cutting down on salt. Salt is present in most natural foods in sufficient quantity to meet the body's requirements. If you must, get yourself some vegetable salt or a salt substitute.

You'll find foods can be perfectly delicious with other seasonings such as herbs and spices. Be creative in your cooking. Any one of the following are wonderful replacements for salt: thyme . . . bay leaves . . . caraway . . . dill weed . . . saffron . . . tarragon . . . peppermint . . . paprika . . . rosemary . . . basil . . . dried or fresh parsley . . . fresh garlic . . . fresh onion . . . lemon or lime juice.

Watch your liquids

Never drink at all during meals. Liquids of any kind tend to dilute the food too much and interfere with the digestive juices. At mealtime, liquids also have a tendency to dilate the stomach, leaving you with that bloated feeling. Except at breakfast, drink your liquids fifteen minutes before meals and two hours after eating. Try to limit your intake of tea and coffee to two cups a day. When you do have tea or coffee, make sure it is weak. Carbonated drinks and soda water should be skipped entirely on this diet.

But the necessary 6 to 8 glasses of drinking water must be taken between meals.

Special help

One of your best allies in the fight against cellulite is iodine. This powerful oxidizing catalyst contributes to the burning up of all the food eaten each day. Iodine is the raw material that powers the thyroid. This gland rules the rate of the metabolism process which burns food for energy. This combustion is important because any food not properly burned up may be stored as unwanted fat which leads to the formation of cellulite. Many delicious foods are rich in iodine. Try to include them in your diet regularly:

Seafood	Bananas
Seaweed	Cabbage
Radishes	Egg yolks
Asparagus	Onion
Carrots	Garlic
Tomatoes	Watercress
Spinach	String beans
Rhubarb	Leeks
Potatoes	Grapes
Peas	Pears
Strawberries	Artichokes
Mushrooms	Brown rice
Lettuce	Turnips

Intelligent snacking

Almost everyone has difficulty confining eating to meals only. And, unfortunately, it is often the between-meal snack foods that contribute to cellulite problems, weight worries or both. The following are foods that will not be detrimental to your cellulite battle, and are tasty as well:

> Fruits
>
> Yogurt
>
> Vegetable juices
>
> Raw vegetables (such as carrots, celery, cucumber, and radishes, all without salt.)
>
> Skim milk (flavored with carob powder if you like. Carob is a delicious chocolate substitute much easier to digest than the real thing.)
>
> Sun dried fruits (such as raisins, prunes, dates and figs—but only if you don't have a weight problem.)
>
> Nuts (just out of their shells—unprocessed and unsalted.)
>
> Seeds (such as sunflower, melon and pumpkin seeds. They are rich in protein and minerals and tasty as well.)

Remember, choose snacks that will not interfere with your desired weight.

The Polluters

There are other foods, however, that *must be strictly avoided*. The following tend to pollute the system and are rarely eliminated without leaving toxic residues. Many are also highly salted.

Pork	Chili con carne
Sausages	Mayonnaise
Bacon	Tuna fish salad °°
Salami	French fries
Pastrami	Potato salad
Pretzels	Chocolate
Potato chips	Cream
Peanut butter°	Alcohol, incl. beer & wine
Olives	Chili (the spice)
Pickles	Tabasco sauce
Salted crackers	Dips
Smoked fish or meat	Sour cream
Blue cheese	Sardines
Fried foods	Pizza
Sundaes	Gravies
Carbonated drinks	Snails
Malteds and shakes	Caviar
Salted nuts	Anchovies
Popcorn	Catsup
Pastries	Sauerkraut
"Gooey" desserts	Frankfurters
TV dinners	Corned beef
Canned soups	Bouillon cubes

°except unsalted peanut butter
°°packed in water, tuna fish, by itself, is acceptable

While not strictly like some other foods, *coffee* intake must be carefully regulated. Coffee addicts needn't fear, however. You can easily find good-tasting substitutes made from the natural extract of cereals, grains, roots and fruits, or you can drink a decaffeinated brand.

Make the most of your meals

Here are some eating guidelines that will help eliminate cellulite and prevent it from coming back:

—*Never eat fast.* Instead, take plenty of time and *chew your food well.* Remember, digestion begins in the mouth.

—Avoid irritations during meals, such as watching TV or disturbing discussions. Stress interferes with digestion. It also frequently causes flatulence because, when you speak too forcefully, you swallow too much air.

—Eat at regular hours as much as possible. The stomach functions best on a schedule.

—If you have a tendency to flatulence, sip liquids through a straw. This will help stop you from swallowing too much air.

—Safeguard your liver with a bland, easy-to-digest diet.

—Always enjoy your meals. Even though there are restrictions, use your imagination to create interesting and tasty menus.

Socializing

When you are invited out, enjoy yourself. If you must accept a drink, make it a straight one—Scotch, rye, bourbon or vodka on the rocks or with water. *One only!* Sip it slowly to make it last. You can have *one* glass of wine. Try to drink it in small sips as you eat. Avoid any after dinner drinks. Remember, this is only for those *special occasions* when you are out in company.

·❈6❈·

Elimination—The Way To
Fight Body Pollution

When the body does a good job of eliminating all of its waste materials, there are none left to "poison" the fatty tissue and turn it into cellulite. Once cellulite has formed, however, proper elimination is even more necessary to flush out the toxic residues. Because maximum elimination is clearly crucial to solving a cellulite problem, all three organs involved—the kidneys, intestines and the skin— must be in superb working order.

How to increase kidney activity

Water is basic in the fight against cellulite. The more water you drink the more active your kidneys will be in cleansing your body of wastes and residues by flushing them out through the urine. Unfortunately, most women with cellulite seldom drink water at all! On the contrary, at least 6 to 8 tall eight-ounce glasses a day are a *must*. Choose tap, spring or non-carbonated mineral water, whichever you like best.

The quantity must be spread out over the day. Many women find it easiest to drink half a glass every hour, or one glass every two hours. *Never try to drink several glasses all at once*. This distends the stomach. The only time you must *not* drink water is with meals. And remember, *this water-drinking program can only be effective when accompanied by a low-salt diet*. If you drink great quantities of water without cutting down on salt, you only aggravate your condition. If you aren't used to drinking this much water, begin with a few glasses a day and gradually build up to the full eight. It will take a few days for your system to respond properly, but done this way, you will never feel bloated.

Even after your cellulite is completely gone, continue to drink at least four full glasses of water each day. It is a wonderfully healthful habit.

Take advantage of evenings and weekends at home to relax and drink plenty of liquids. Stretch your feet out in front of you, cushion your back and recline at ease. It's a comfortable position—and one in which your kidneys function best. Read, watch TV or simply relax while you drink.

An alternative

Natural diuretics can be taken in place of water for those unable to drink the quantities recommended, or simply as a variation. Invaluable, these diuretics increase the volume of urine, exactly what is needed to help flush out waste residues. But this should be done *naturally*, rather than with the water pills discussed before. Special *tisanes* (herbal teas) can be used for this purpose. Because they are totally natural, you can drink as much as you like. There are many kinds available. Experiment to see which you like best. At first you may find the taste a bit strange, but these teas are well worth getting used to, because they help to cleanse the system thoroughly.

Prepare a fresh pot of tea each day and drink at least four full cups. As with water, don't drink the tea with meals, but at other times during the day. You can add a *soupçon* of honey and a few drops of lemon if you like.

Here are some recipes for diuretic teas:

CORN SILK TEA:

*Place 1½ ounces of corn silk
in 1 quart of water. Boil for a few minutes.
Strain and sip slowly.*

MEADOW-SWEET TEA:

*Steep 2 ounces of meadow-sweet
in 1 quart of very hot water.
Strain. Serve hot.*

CHERRY STEMS TEA:

*Put ¾ ounce of cherry stems
in 1 quart of water. Boil for a few minutes.
Strain and pour out.*

HORSETAIL TEA:

*Place ½ ounce of horsetail
in 1 quart of water. Bring to a boil, and
simmer for 25 minutes.
Strain and drink.*

You can find all of these natural ingredients at a health food store, or at an herb dealer. Two of them are often in your very own kitchen—corn silk and cherry stems. When you shuck ears of corn, save the protective silk covering. And when you serve cherries, don't discard the stems. Let both of these natural remedies dry as you would garden herbs, and keep them for use as teas later on.

If you work in an office, it might be easier for you to use the packaged herbal diuretic varieties. But do try to use the individual teas whenever possible.

Diuretic foods

Aside from the teas, there are many solid foods which have diuretic properties: asparagus . . . pumpkin . . . leeks . . . cabbage (preferably the red or green curly variety) . . . watercress . . . fennel . . . onion . . . grapefruit (particularly effective when eaten first thing in the morning) . . . apples . . . radishes . . . grapes . . . pineapples. Cumin, the spice, and sage used to flavor food, have helpful diuretic properties. Try to include these foods in your diet in solid form, cooked or raw, or as juices made in your extractor. They'll get right after your cellulite!

Constipation

Constipation is a big problem that is interrelated with cellulite. When you are constipated and cannot eliminate properly, the body is forced to retain toxic wastes. So, aside from being unpleasant and uncomfortable, constipation is often responsible for creating cellulite.

What are some of the causes of constipation?

Sedentariness and lack of exercise—physical activity aids digestion and keeps the muscles in tone, particularly those of the abdominal wall which assist in the elimination process.

Poor posture—slumping "crowds" the organs, cramps their ease of activity and puts undesirable pressure on the intestines.

Poor nutrition—modern eating habits rely heavily on over-processed and devitalized foods such as white bread and white sugar. This diet too often lacks fresh fruit and vegetables.

Not enough water—daily intake of water greatly facilitates the bowel processes.

Tension—nervous tension constricts and tightens the muscles, including those directly responsible for bowel movements.

Laxatives—habitual use becomes habit forming, causing normal bowel reflexes to grow lazy and, eventually, unable to act on their own. Laxatives can never cure irregularity. At best, they can offer temporary relief. At worst, they can practically ruin the body's natural ability to eliminate waste.

The natural way to fight constipation

A well-balanced diet and a program of proper exercise is the best way to prevent irregularity and to fight constipation naturally. Drinking large amounts of water also encourages proper bowel functioning. Many people find it helpful to drink a glass of fresh water first thing each morning. For others, warm water is even more effective. Still others like to add lemon juice to the water. Experiment with all three. You'll discover which works best for you.

The prune is another of nature's most valuable elimination aids. Try drinking a glass of unsweetend prune juice "spiked" with the juice of half a lemon when you get up in the morning. Or soak some prunes in water overnight and eat them at breakfast. Straight from the box, prunes are a delightful dessert or TV snack.

Another old-fashioned and proven remedy is a tablespoonful of pure, natural vegetable oil taken before eating in the morning and just before bedtime at night. Try corn, safflower or wheat germ oil. They are not at all unpleasant and leave no after-taste. Never use mineral oil because it depletes the body of vitamins.

Some herbs are quite valuable as natural laxatives. Senakot is one suggestion. Swiss Kriss, a combination of laxative herbs, is another. Add a teaspoon of Swiss Kriss to a cup of boiling water, steep for three minutes and strain. Add a teaspoonful of honey, a few drops of lemon juice, if you like, and drink just before going to bed.

Include some natural laxative foods in your diet

Let nature help keep you regular by eating these foods often:

Honey—a mild, natural laxative which should always be used in place of sugar. You can eat it straight from the jar whenever you have a hunger pang or feel your energy getting low.

Blackstrap molasses—take just before retiring. Stir a tablespoonful into a glass of milk.

Yeast—use dried brewers' yeast generously every day because this is rich in B vitamins, essential for the maintenance of good muscle tone in the intestinal tract. Mix it (in the blender is best) with fruit or vegetable juices to make it more palatable.

Wheat germ—another natural laxative very high in vitamins and protein. Use plenty of it throughout the day by sprinkling it on cereals, fruits, soups, salads, etc.

Yogurt—a form of cultured milk containing bacteria active in the synthesis of the B vitamins so crucial to proper elimination. Aside from making a delicious dessert, yogurt can be eaten any time during the day as a mini-meal or a healthful snack.

Also be sure you eat plenty of fresh fruits and vegetables every day—and green, leafy salads, dressed with pure, natural vegetable oil. Natural aids to elimination are not only effective and valuable, but often quite delicious.

One proven exercise to aid elimination

While all exercising helps the body to perform at its best, there is a specific exercise geared to giving the elimination process an effective push. It's the *Abdominal Contraction*, a completely natural movement which prevents and relieves irregularity. It also increases the firmness and tone of the abdominal muscles which are so instrumental in good elimination. As an added plus, the *Abdominal Contraction* helps to reduce a flabby or heavy waistline.

Follow these directions:

1. Standing with feet a few inches apart, bend your knees slightly. Lean forward and place hands on your thighs, with fingers pointing inward.

2. Empty your lungs, exhaling all the air through your mouth. (The lungs must be kept empty throughout this exercise.)

3. Drawing your stomach in and upward, trying to bring it against the spine, contract your abdominal muscles. Hold for one second, to a mental count of one, two, three.

4. Let your abdomen "pop" out in a brisk, but gentle, movement.

5. Without inhaling, repeat pulling your stomach in and up again. Hold this for one second again and then let go. Do the in-and-out movement 4 or 5 times without inhaling any air. This is one "set" of *Abdominal Contractions.*

6. Stand up straight and inhale. Rest for a few minutes until you are breathing normally again.

7. Return to the starting position and repeat the whole procedure. 5 "sets" are your goal at the beginning.

Always remember to exhale *before* doing the contractions and never allow any air to enter the lungs *while* doing movements. Perform as many sets as you can, but don't force yourself. When you first start, you may only be able to do one. In time you will become accustomed to the exercise and will easily be able to do 10 or more sets! Try doing the *Abdominal Contractions* in front of a mirror. When you see a great hollow in your abdomen, you will know that you are doing it correctly.

The *Abdominal Contraction* must always be done on an empty stomach, preferably when you get up in the morning. One exception when the problem is particularly serious: A few minutes before doing the exercise, try drinking a glass of water containing the juice of half a lemon.

The skin—an organ of elimination

Through perspiration, the skin performs an important elimination function. The body has about two million sweat glands that are helpful in the fight against cellulite because they work together to expel many impurities. The more wastes they expel, the better. There are several ways to increase perspiration. One of the most effective is the sauna.

Exactly what is a sauna?

The dry heat sauna bath originated in Finland centuries ago. Today it is practically a national institution. Not only does every Finnish hotel have sauna equipment, but almost every home has similar facilities. Truly integral to Finnish life, the sauna may be anywhere in a house or apartment, or even outdoors in a garden, preferably by a lake. Inside, walls are paneled with unpainted pine wood which absorbs moisture from the air. A series of benches or platforms, also of unpainted pine, line the walls. If the sauna is located outdoors, it usually looks like a small, attractive cabin.

Inside the sauna, a stove topped with volcanic stones emits heat varying between 150 to 180 degrees F. A little water is poured on the heated stones from time to time. Humidity is less than 10 percent.

Customarily, as they begin to perspire heavily, the Finns start hitting themselves with leafy birch branches to help expand the capillaries and stimulate circulation. After about 10 to 20 minutes they take a cold shower, scrubbing vigorously. If the sauna is in the country, the Finns take a dip in a cool lake or stream. In winter, they roll in the snow or carve a hole in an iced-covered lake and jump in! Actually the sauna is complete with one session of heat followed by a cold shower or swim, but most Finns go through both steps two or three times! After drying off, a half hour of rest and relaxation is a must. The Finns love the sauna, and they are a nation of healthy, lively people with beautiful skins to prove it.

COURTESY OF THE FINNISH NATIONAL TOURIST OFFICE

How can sauna help eliminate cellulite?

The abundant perspiration created by a session of sauna (as much as two or three pints), cleanses the skin deeply, carrying away many impurities and toxic substances. This deep-pore cleansing allows the skin to breathe better, and the action of the sauna followed by a cold shower greatly stimulates circulation. The sauna is also a wonderful way to relax and is very effective in promoting a deep, sound sleep. (Avoid a sauna in the case of high blood pressure or heart trouble.)

You should take a sauna bath once or twice a week while working on your cellulite problem. It's best after exercise. If you can, drink a cup of hot diuretic tea before entering the sauna. The cold shower that follows closes the pores and brings circulation back to normal. (The water should be as *cool* as you can stand it.)

Sauna is a good practice to continue at least once a week, even after your cellulite is gone. Installing a home model sauna is well worth the investment. There are many on the market from which to choose, ranging from small portable units to full-scale, prefabricated models.

Although the dry heat of a sauna is preferable, a regular steam bath also encourages perspiration. Like the sauna, it should be followed by a cool shower. Here, too, there are many models on the market for use at home.

What other ways can perspiration be induced?

Remember going to the beach and getting "buried" in the sand? This childhood game can be very helpful to you in your anti-cellulite program. We call the grown-up version the *Dry Sand Bath*. When you cover yourself with warm sand, you are actually creating a natural sauna. A dry sand bath works just like a conventional sauna, causing much perspiration and, consequently, eliminating impurities and toxic wastes. It also dilates the capillaries and stimulates circulation. In addition, it is immensely relaxing. The next time you're at the beach, try the *Dry Sand Bath* for 10 to 30 minutes and follow with a cool dip in the ocean. You'll find this a delightful experience!

Exercising, rowing and jogging, while dressed in a sweat suit or warm woolen clothes, are also examples of effective ways to stimulate perspiration.

Friction rub

Surface friction brings nourishment to the skin. By drawing blood to the surface (where it can help flush out trapped wastes in the cellulite deposits) friction rubs help deliver food nutrients needed by the skin cells. Surface stimulation also increases the flow of blood throughout the body. It soothes nerves. And, by shedding the dulling dead surface cells, friction helps the skin breathe more fully and improves its texture.

Wet or dry, the friction rub is equally effective. For most women, it is simply more convenient when combined with a bath or shower. Once you have soaped up, rub your whole body vigorously with a natural bristle brush or a loofah. Work up and down on your arms and legs, in circular motions around back and tummy, for about two minutes. Then concentrate specifically on the cellulite areas for a few more minutes, rubbing until they become really pink. Finish off with a hand spray, hosing cool water from your feet on up your body. If you don't have a hand spray, gradually reduce the temperature of your shower water to cool and rinse completely.

Aside from helping to break down cellulite bulges, the dry friction rub leaves the skin so smooth that practically every French woman includes it as part of her daily beauty routine. Use a dry loofah (mitt or strap) and rub as you would in the tub. Don't apply too much pressure. The dry rub makes the skin really pink faster than the wet rub. If your skin is extremely sensitive, dampen the loofah just slightly. The pinkness is your way of knowing that the blood has come to the surface of the skin.

Once you've become accustomed to the dry loofah rub, you can advance to a coarser friction mitt made of twisted wool and horsehair (imported from France or Germany). If your druggist doesn't carry it, he can probably order one for you. Give yourself a 5 or 6 minute dry friction rub every day, concentrating on the cellulite areas until they become blushing red. Even when cellulite is no longer a problem, continue your daily friction rub, as French women do. It's quite invigorating and gives you beautiful, baby-smooth skin.

COURTESY OF THE FRENCH GOVERNMENT TOURIST OFFICE

·❄7❄·

Breathe Your Way To Cellulite Control

Vital to all living things, the simple act of breathing has added significance for those plagued with cellulite. Breathing, or drawing in oxygen and exhaling carbon dioxide, purifies the blood and helps burn up the toxic wastes that are the "raw materials" of cellulite.

Unfortunately, very few of us know how to breathe properly. With each breath, we fill our lungs to only one-eighth of their capacity. Full, deep breathing, on the other hand, produces higher oxygenation which burns up greater amounts of waste materials. Because this burning helps dissociate cellulite, we must aim at inhaling and exhaling as much as possible.

Few people realize that breathing is actually a form of nourishment. The body must be fed oxygen in order to function. You can exist without food for over a month. You can do without water for almost a week. Without oxygen, you cannot exist for more than a few minutes. If you want a slim, trim body, free of lumpy cellulite bulges, you may have to change your breathing habits. You must recognize breathing as a crucial, nourishing, life-sustaining process.

If you change your breathing habits, you can change your entire pattern of living. Learning to breathe deeply will help you look and feel immeasurably better. It will revitalize your complexion and help to soothe your nerves. If you breathe deeply and fully, you stand a better chance of remaining calm and in full control of your emotions. If, on the other hand, you breathe in shallow, hurried gasps, your mind becomes agitated and you are more likely to become upset. No wonder Yoga experts insist upon correct breathing as the first step toward peace of mind!

Yoga breathing exercises are particularly effective in developing good breathing habits and maximum lung capacity. Because of the increasing amount of fumes and impurities that make their way into our lungs these days, the kind of breathing that Yoga exercises produce is practically a necessity to counteract the effects of pollution. They correct the shallow sort of breathing that leads to body devitalization, chronic fatigue, lack of energy and even to mental depression. The *Complete Breath,* described below, lets you re-educate yourself to breathe in the most healthful way possible.

Complete Breath

1. Place both hands on rib cage. Exhale completely.
2. Inhale very slowly through your nose, counting to 5 until your abdomen feels filled with air.
3. Continue inhaling slowly, counting another 5 and expand your chest, until it, too, is filled with air.
4. Hold the air to a count of 5.
5. Exhale very slowly through your nose, counting to 10 and push with your stomach to completely remove the air from your lungs.

In the beginning, it might take you no longer than 6 to 10 seconds. A *Complete Breath* takes about 25 seconds from start to finish. When you hold your ribs, you can feel the expansion as air fills your lungs. You can feel your body responding. Once you develop your breathing capacity fully, you can feel it without using your hands.

This kind of deep breathing, which brings a greater amount of oxygen into your system than shallow breathing, is instrumental in the treatment of cellulite. Practice it for a few minutes every day to purify your blood. You can deep breathe any time, even while doing something else. And, whenever you're tired or tense, a two- or three-minute session will make you feel relaxed and refreshed.

Here's another invaluable breathing exercise. Called the *Cleansing Breath*, it loosens harmful impurities from the lung tissue, and enables you to expel them. It also strengthens the abdomen and the diaphragm. And it's a great way to clear your mind! Try it as a wake-up exercise in the morning—or during the day whenever you feel sluggish or tired.

Cleansing Breath

1. While expanding your abdomen as fast as you can, inhale as much air as possible.

2. Quickly, with one sudden movement, pull your abdomen in while you expel the air from your lungs through your nostrils as powerfully as possible. When done correctly, this produces a hissing sound.

It's important that this exercise be done with a definite rhythmic pattern. You can begin as slowly as you wish, gradually increasing the tempo. Ideally, each *Cleansing Breath* should take one or two seconds. They should follow continuously, without pausing between each one. Try to do 10 in a row. When you have completed one series of *Cleansing Breaths*, take one *Complete Breath* to finish the routine.

Try to develop the habit of doing both *Complete* and *Cleansing Breath* exercises every day. The following four *Special Breathing Exercises* or *Sun Greeting* are additional helps to get yourself breathing more naturally and to increase the necessary supply of oxygen in the blood.

1. Standing with your arms close to your body, breathe in while you slowly raise your arms straight overhead. Breathe out while you reach down and touch the floor.

2. Stand straight, with arms out in front of you, shoulder high. Breathe in while you slowly open your arms. Breathe out while you bring your arms back together in front of you.

These four *Special Breathing Exercises* should be done slowly, and repeated 6 to 10 times each.

3. Standing with feet apart, breathe in while you bring your arms straight overhead. Twist your torso to the right and breathe out while you slowly bend down and touch your right foot. Slowly raise your arms while breathing in. Twist your torso to the left and breathe out while you slowly bend down and touch your left foot.

4. Standing straight, breathe in while you slowly bring your arms straight overhead. Breathe out as you lower yourself to a squatting position as illustrated.

2. Breathe in deeply, raise your arms high above your head and reach backward as far as you can.

3. Bend forward, reaching down as far as possible and exhale. It doesn't matter whether or not you touch the floor, so don't strain yourself. Remember to keep your legs together.

1. Stand up straight with legs together, elbows close to the body and hands together in "praying" position. Breathe in deeply, feel your chest expand, then exhale.

Another deep breathing exercise, taken from Yoga, is the *Sun Greeting*, an excellent combination of exercise and deep breathing that will improve your circulation, firm your muscles and soothe your mind. Done regularly it will tone up your digestive organs and improve elimination —especially valuable to those of you who suffer from constipation and poor digestion. Done in the morning, it will help get your day started by "revving" up your circulation. As an evening exercise, it will help to relieve nervous tension and prepare you for a good night's sleep.

Doing all the movements as slowly as possible, go through the *Sun Greeting* once or twice, morning and evening.

4. Then, with hands on
the floor, assume a partial
kneeling position. Breathe
in as you bend your left
leg up to your chest,
while extending your
right leg backward. Keep
your head up.

5. Exhale as you stretch
both legs out together,
extending your left leg so that
your body is supported
by your hands and toes.
Keep your body stiff.

6. Without breathing
in, lower yourself
down, resting your chest
and forehead on the floor.

7. Breathe in and push your trunk up by straightening your arms. Keep your head up and back, with your thighs remaining on the floor. If you cannot straighten your arms completely, don't force yourself.

8. Without moving your hands or feet, bring your hips up as high as possible to form a triangle. Let your head hang down between your shoulders. Exhale.

9. Bring your right leg under your body and lift your head up. Breathe in. (This Step is similar to Step 4 except that the position of the leg is reversed.)

10. Keeping your hands on the floor, breathe out while you bring both feet together, straightening your legs as much as possible. Again, don't force yourself.

11. As you breathe in deeply, straighten up, bringing your arms up and backward as far as you can.

12. Breathe out while returning your hands to the starting position— elbows close to the body with hands together.

If you feel a bit tired after doing the *Sun Greeting*, take a few deep breaths and relax.

Simple tips on breathing to fight cellulite

There are many ways you can use oxidation to help you get rid of cellulite. First of all, try to be more active. If you are, you will automatically breathe more deeply. Pass up the bus or subway and walk or jog whenever possible. If you have a desk job, get up and stretch every hour or so. And don't keep everything at your fingertips. You'll be forced to get up and go fetch from time to time. Secondly, do your best to avoid smoke-filled atmospheres. If you have been in a smoky night club or close, stagnant theatre, take a few *Deep* and *Cleansing Breaths* to combat the harmful effects as soon as you can find some clean air!

Because of all the pollutants and noxious fumes in the city, you should try to get some fresh, clean country air into your lungs as often as possible. If you're lucky enough to live near a seashore, take advantage of the salt air whenever possible. Pay particular attention to breathing properly whenever you are at the beach. Salt air helps greatly in the oxidation of impurities.

Your skin breathes too

Lungs are not the only organs that breathe. Responsible for about one-seventh of your body's total breathing, your skin is constantly engaged in absorbing oxygen and eliminating carbon dioxide as well as other impurities. So let it breathe! Try to avoid wearing clothes made from 100 percent synthetic materials. These seem to hamper the skin from breathing properly. Change into something loose when you are around the house so that air can circulate freely about your body.

Take *air baths* whenever possible, wearing absolutely nothing so that your skin can really get a good workout, away from any confinement.

If you always remember that breathing is a form of nourishment, you are bound to improve your breathing habits instinctively.

·❈8❈·

Exercise—The Allover Cellulite Attack

Life styles of today practically exclude consistent physical work. Everyday activity usually is not enough to maintain muscle elasticity and tone. Insufficient exercise causes the body to change significantly and to lose its shape. Muscles start to atrophy. Tissue texture modifies. Firmness gives way to flabbiness and cellulite.

Unlike organs that work around the clock (heart, liver and stomach), voluntary muscles function only when specifically called upon. But they have a direct effect upon the way other organs perform. Some muscles help to keep organs in place. Abdominal muscles, for example, support the viscera. It is vital that all muscles be kept in good condition.

Think of exercise as joyful—something to look forward to. Regular exercise gives you that incomparable feeling of well-being. It can make you calm, graceful and poised. When walking, your body will feel wonderfully light and free. You'll step proudly with a great deal of self-confidence instead of just dragging along. You'll have control of your body. You'll feel alive and fit!

What exercise can do for a cellulite condition

The body's energy is supplied by food. After digestion, blood and lymph carry nourishment to the tissues where it is immediately used for movement or stored for later use. These nourishing materials are burned up during the breathing process. When oxidation is insufficient, as it is in a sedentary person, toxic substances are not burned up and remain in the tissues. These substances, such as uric acid, can be quite detrimental to health. Muscle training or toning—that is *exercise*—provides the increased oxidation that can accelerate the vital burning process and reinstate physiological equilibrium that has been impaired by inactivity or excess food.

Exercise improves circulation, boosts elimination, improves the functioning of the body's organs—particularly those involved in digestion and respiration—and reduces nervous tension. All these conditions are necessary to lose cellulite.

Not all exercise works on cellulite. This requires a planned group of movements, as described later. Some of these movements help to dissipate cellulite by their massage action. Others increase circulation, thus insuring drainage and elimination of loosened cellulite wastes.

Never force any exercise. Be careful not to strain yourself while performing each movement to the best of your ability. During exercise try to concentrate on what you are doing instead of thinking "let's get it over with." This will make all your movements more effective. With gradual practice, you will be able to perform all of the exercises with ease.

If you have not exercised for a long time, curb your initial enthusiasm. *Do not over-exercise!* You will only become exhausted and discouraged—so discouraged, as a matter of fact, that you might give up your exercise program completely and never return to it. It's easy to determine what your limit is. Your body will tell you.

You will probably experience some soreness the first day. Don't let that stop you. In just a few days, you'll be able to do the exercises without any soreness at all.

How long should you keep up an exercise program?

Even when you have re-shaped your body and are free of cellulite, continue exercising. Would you ever think of brushing your teeth for only a month or two and expect them to stay in fine condition? Naturally not. The same goes for your whole body. Exercise should be a part of your routine for the rest of your life. Time spent exercising will be time well spent. Muscular flexibility and the ability to move gracefully diminish with age. However, regular exercise will help you stay agile and graceful throughout life.

Key to exercising for cellulite

There are no "miracle exercises" to fight cellulite but the right ones can help. When performed properly, those suggested at the end of this chapter will definitely accelerate the loss of cellulite. Some of them probably will be familiar to you. You may even have tried them before but with no appreciable results. Key things to remember when exercising are *coordination* of the suggested movements and *deep breathing*. The coordinated movements are specially planned to make the most of muscle work. Deep breathing increases oxidation.

To make your program as simple as possible, the exercises are divided into groups according to specific areas of the body. If you need work on more than one area, select a few exercises from each group. You can alternate groups on different days, if you prefer. Either way, *devote at least 15 minutes each day* to the program.

Start each exercise session with a few stretching and rotating movements to loosen up and remove tension and stiffness from the spinal area. This is particularly important if you have not exercised in a long time. In the beginning, concentrate primarily on doing the movements properly. It's far better to.do a *few* of the exercises *right* than to do *all* of them *wrong*. Work at a medium pace, neither too fast nor too slow, unless otherwise specified. And take some time during each exercise session for a few *Complete Breaths* as suggested in Chapter 7.

Correct breathing and exercise

To do any exercise properly, you should exhale when you bend or bring your limbs close to the body. You should inhale every time you stretch, lift or raise your body or any part of it.

Wind Up Stand, feet slightly apart, hands on hips. Rotate from the waist, slowly making a complete circle from right to left, 5 times. Reverse directions, going from left to right 5 times.

Limber Up Stand straight, feet apart. Raise hands overhead first, then bend down, touching fingers to floor if you can. Bounce from the waist until you feel loose, about 3 times. Repeat whole motion 5 times.

Number one cellulite problem

THIGHS are the most susceptible area. They develop cellulite faster and more thoroughly than any other part of the body. Upper thighs bulge, insides sag and backs become rippled. All parts suffer the effects of cellulite. Sitting is responsible for much of this because it compresses the tissues and restricts circulation. Wearing a girdle and crossing the legs are both extremely detrimental for the thighs as they also cut down on free and easy circulation. The following group of exercises specifically for thighs, aims to restore good circulation to flush out the residues causing cellulite. Like the upper arms, the insides of the thighs are also very prone to flab and need constant attention to keep them from sagging out of shape, whether they are affected by cellulite or not.

1. Sit on the floor and bring your feet together as illustrated. Rock from side to side. If you like, you can put your hands on your knees to keep your balance. Rock to a count of 40.

2. Sit, hands on the floor, slightly behind you, knees bent. Touch both knees to the floor on the right side, then to the left side. Touch 20 times on each side.

3. Lying on your back, one arm overhead, roll to the side as illustrated. Repeat 15 to 20 times. Then do the same thing rolling to the other side.

4. Sit on the floor and bring your knees up.

4-A. Now roll over, without knees touching the floor.

4-B. Extend legs in front of you. Then bend knees again and roll over on the other side. Extend legs. Do 10 to 15 times, reversing sides.

These first four exercises act like a powerful massage. They will help break down that "bump" on the upper side of the thigh. Start off by doing them 15 to 20 times. Then increase to as many as you can, anywhere from 50 to 100.

Lying on your side, bring one leg up as illustrated.
Lower and repeat 10 times. Then roll over and do the
other leg. To make this movement effective for the inside
thigh as well, fasten light weights around your
ankles. Do the movement very slowly.

Lie on your back and
bring both legs
straight up. Spread the
legs and slowly
bring them back
together in a scissor
movement. The
movement is a lot
more effective when
done with weights
fastened on the ankles,
as illustrated.
(For inside thigh.)
Repeat 10 times.

Sit on the floor, as illustrated, and slowly raise your knees while resisting with your elbows. (For inside thigh.)

Note: For these three exercises, you must *feel* the muscles on the inside thigh working, pulling and contracting. So do the movements *very slowly.*

Stand up, holding on to the back of a chair to keep
your balance. Bend your left knee and raise your leg up to
the side and back, as shown. Hold this position for a few
seconds. Then lower the leg. Repeat 5 to 10 times.
Then do the same exercise with your right leg.

Lie on the floor and bring the soles of your
feet together as illustrated.

Then bring the knees together, as shown. Hold for
a few seconds. Repeat 10 times.

B. Then, in one
continuous movement, swing
leg out to the side.

A. On all fours swing leg up.

C. Raise leg again and bring back to starting
position. Repeat 5 to 10 times on each side.

Lying on your back, swing your hips off the floor, as illustrated, and *slowly* bicycle in the air, 20 to 30 times making large circles. It is extremely important that you do this exercise at the end of your session. This reverses the pull of gravity of the body's fluids and drains the residues released by the preceding movements.

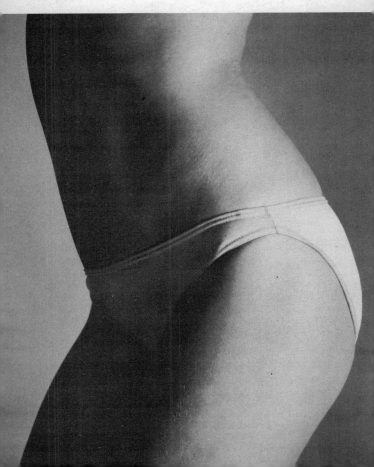

Second cellulite nuisance

HIPS AND BUTTOCKS are only slightly less prone to cellulite than the thighs, and for the same reasons. Neither is exercised very much in the normal course of day-to-day living. People simply sit too much. As time goes by, the muscles in the hips and buttocks grow flabby and start to sag. Sitting also clogs circulation and compresses the tissues inordinately—a perfect situation to breed cellulite. Even without cellulite, too much inactivity flattens and widens the entire area so that it appears out of proportion.

Again, think of the first four exercises as a terrific massage that will help break down cellulite on the buttocks and hips.

Again, think of the first four exercises as a terrific
massage that will help break
down cellulite on the buttocks and hips.

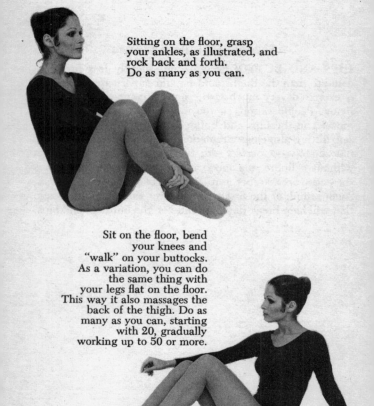

Sitting on the floor, grasp
your ankles, as illustrated, and
rock back and forth.
Do as many as you can.

Sit on the floor, bend
your knees and
"walk" on your buttocks.
As a variation, you can do
the same thing with
your legs flat on the floor.
This way it also massages the
back of the thigh. Do as
many as you can, starting
with 20, gradually
working up to 50 or more.

Kneel down. Try to sit
on the floor on your right side.
Then lift up and sit on the
left side. Use your
arms, as illustrated, to keep
your balance. Repeat
10 to 15 times on each side.

Lying on the floor with
arms straight out, bend your
knees bringing feet toward
buttocks. Lower knees to
touch the floor, first on the
right side then on the left
side. Repeat 10 to 15 times.

DERRIÈRE-FIRMERS

Stand with arms out
in front of you or hold on to
a chair. Bending your knees,
lower yourself slowly
to a squatting position, then
slowly raise up.
Repeat 5 to 10 times.

Kneeling down on all fours,
raise one leg, as illustrated.
Hold to a count of 5, then lower.
Repeat 5 to 10 times, then
do the same thing with the other
leg. Firms the buttocks.

Lie on your side and swing one leg forward,
then back as far as you can. Hold to the count of 3.
Point toes. Repeat 10 times. Roll over to the
other side and repeat 10 times.

Lie on stomach, chin on hands. Raise one leg up as high
as you can. Hold to a count of 5,
then lower. Repeat 5 to 10 times, then change legs.

Lie down with arms stretched along your body. Bend your
knees and slowly raise your buttocks to the position
illustrated, keeping feet flat on the floor. Hold for a count of 5
then slowly lower. Repeat 5 times.

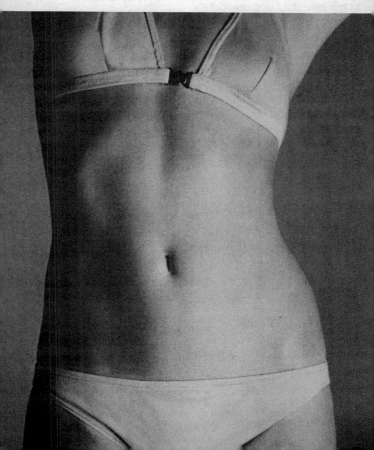

Nasty and noticeable

The **WAISTLINE**, or abdominal region, is made of very powerful muscles which hold the visceral organs in place. When these muscles relax, whether due to poor posture or even wearing a girdle, the abdominal wall gives, leaving the area sagging, flabby and protruding, often invaded by cellulite. The waist thickens and enlarges, changing a woman's entire appearance. Buttocks seem to flatten. Thighs lose their proportion, often looking like sticks compared to the enlarged waist. Such devastation of the abdominal muscles is unhealthy as well as unattractive. It results in digestive problems; interferes with the assimilation process; disturbs elimination and causes constipation.

Stand with feet apart and
arms outstretched.
Twist torso from side to
side. Repeat 10 to 20
times on each side.

Stand with feet apart,
hands clasped behind the
head with elbows straight
back. Bend down,
elbows level with waist, to
the right and then to
the left. Repeat 10 to 15
times on each side.

With feet apart and arms
outstretched, touch your
foot with the opposite
hand, as illustrated.
Bend, touch right hand to
left foot, straighten up
and reverse. Bend,
touch left hand to right
foot. Repeat 10 times
with both
arm/leg combinations.

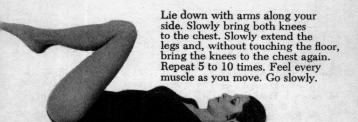

Lie down with arms along your side. Slowly bring both knees to the chest. Slowly extend the legs and, without touching the floor, bring the knees to the chest again. Repeat 5 to 10 times. Feel every muscle as you move. Go slowly.

Sit on the floor, hands on your hips, feet flat on the floor, knees bent. Slowly lean back as far as you can without losing your balance, keeping feet as flat as possible, and then slowly return to starting position. Repeat 5 to 10 times. Your abdominal muscles shape up as they contract to maintain balance in this position.

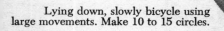

Lying down, slowly bicycle using large movements. Make 10 to 15 circles.

Note: Do all the movements *very slowly*. Always remember to keep your *back* absolutely *flat* on the floor whenever you are doing movements lying down.

Sit on a chair and bring
your knees up, as
illustrated. Then slowly
straighten out
legs. Repeat 10 times.

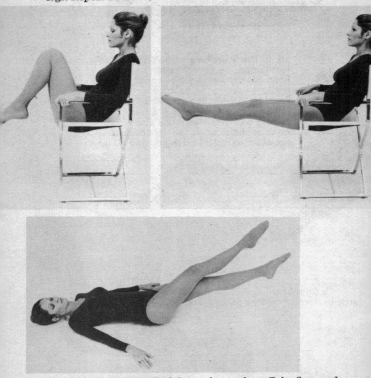

Lie flat on the floor. Raise both legs a few inches off the floor and
do slow, criss-cross scissor movements. Repeat 10 times. Feel
the pull on your stomach muscles as they work to keep legs up.

Lying flat on the floor, clasp your hands behind your head and slowly lift your torso. Bend forward as far as you can. Then slowly return to the floor. To make it easier, you can anchor your feet under a piece of heavy furniture or have someone hold your feet down. Repeat 10 times.

Lie down flat on the floor with arms along your body. Slowly raise both legs straight up. Then slowly lower them to the floor, always keeping knees stiff. Repeat 10 times.

Lie down on your back and slowly bring one knee to your chest. Straighten this leg while bringing the other knee to the chest. Do this continuously with your feet off the floor, and toes pointed to keep your legs pulling on the stomach muscles. Repeat 10 times.

What you don't see

The feminine **BACK** is truly beautiful. Muscles flanking the spine on both sides form a lovely kind of "hollow"— when it's in good shape! Cellulite on the lower back thickens the waist and changes the shape of the hips. On the upper back at the bra line, it results in unsightly bulges, particularly unattractive in a bathing suit or under a tight dress. Beauty aside, muscles give the spine its flexibility, so it's important that they be well-exercised. In addition, the back is highly susceptible to muscular tension pains. Frequent backaches and even severe pains are very common complaints. Proper exercise is the best means to prevent these problems.

For the first three exercises, use a pair of dumbbells, 2 or 3 pounds each. Substitute books or socks filled with something heavy like sand or rocks, weighing 2 or 3 pounds.

2. Stand with feet apart, knees stiff, arms along your body. Bend down, as illustrated, keeping elbows stiff. Slowly bring both arms up behind the back. Hold this position to a count of 3, then bring the arms down. Repeat 10 times. Excellent for the upper back where the bra bulge begins.

1. Stand with feet apart, arms straight overhead. Bend down and bring dumbbell between legs as far back as possible, keeping knees stiff. Repeat 10 times.

3. Stand with feet apart, arms along your body. Bring both arms behind your back. Hold the position, count to 3 and bring arms back to your sides. Repeat 10 times. This is also helpful for upper back bulge.

4. Stand with feet apart and hands clasped behind the head. Bend down, as illustrated, keeping elbows straight. Repeat 10 times.

These four exercises
are performed with a stick or heavy bar.

Begin as illustrated.
Slowly straighten up.
Then slowly lower the
bar to the floor.
Repeat 10 times.

Start by bending from
the waist and holding
the bar near the floor.
Slowly bring bar to
chest, as you force the
elbows back. Then slowly
lower the bar to
the floor. Repeat 10
times. Make certain you
feel the contraction in
the upper back as
you squeeze the elbows.

Start by holding the bar straight overhead. Slowly lower it behind your shoulders to the position shown. Count to 5 and raise again. Repeat 10 times—each time experiencing the movement in your upper back—and the release of tension.

Holding the bar on your shoulders, slowly bend forward. Straighten up slowly. Repeat 10 times. This helps to release kinks along the spine as it works on the lower back.

Give them your all

KNEES, unfortunately, thicken and lump easily and insidiously. The resulting hard mass completely obliterates the graceful contour of the knees. Few exercises affect the knees directly, so a combination of slapping and friction movement is necessary. Cellulite, if it does affect the knee, is generally attributed to poor local circulation caused by standing too long or sitting in a position in which the knee is bent for long periods of time.

Lie on your back, knees bent and feet flat on the floor. Slap the
knees together at a regular, even pace. Starting with 20 for
the first time, do as many as you can, eventually working up to 100.

Still on the floor, bring
both legs straight up,
as illustrated, and again slap
the knees together.
Repeat 20 to 50 times.

In the same position, rub the knees together as you circle your legs in bicycle movements. Repeat 20 to 50 times.

Flab haven

UPPER ARMS are a favorite place for flab to form, both on the inside and at the point where the arms join the upper back—the well-known "bra bulge." With little exercise, upper arms deteriorate rapidly. Lack of muscle tone brings about sagging and provides hospitality for the formation of cellulite. Because the tissues of the upper arm are delicate, constant attention is imperative to prevent flab from becoming a problem. Using light dumbbell weights can help tone up the area. So can specific Yoga movements.

The first two exercises call for the use of light dumbbells (about 3 pounds) or the alternatives suggested for the back exercises.

From the position illustrated, slowly raise and lower the arm straight overhead. Repeat 10 to 15 times with each arm.

Begin in the position illustrated. Then slowly extend the arm all the way out to the side. Bend back. Repeat 10 to 15 times, each arm.

The next exercises which are taken from Yoga, use the body itself as a resistance.

Standing with arms along the body, reach your right hand over your shoulder, your left hand up your back, trying to make the fingers touch. If you can, try to clasp your hands in a firm grip. Once in the position, hold it motionless to the count of 5. Then slowly lower the arms. Repeat 3 times with each arm.

Sitting or standing, with arms along the body, slowly bring both arms behind your back, trying to make the palms of both hands meet. Hold the position motionless to the count of 5. Then slowly lower the arms and repeat 3 times.

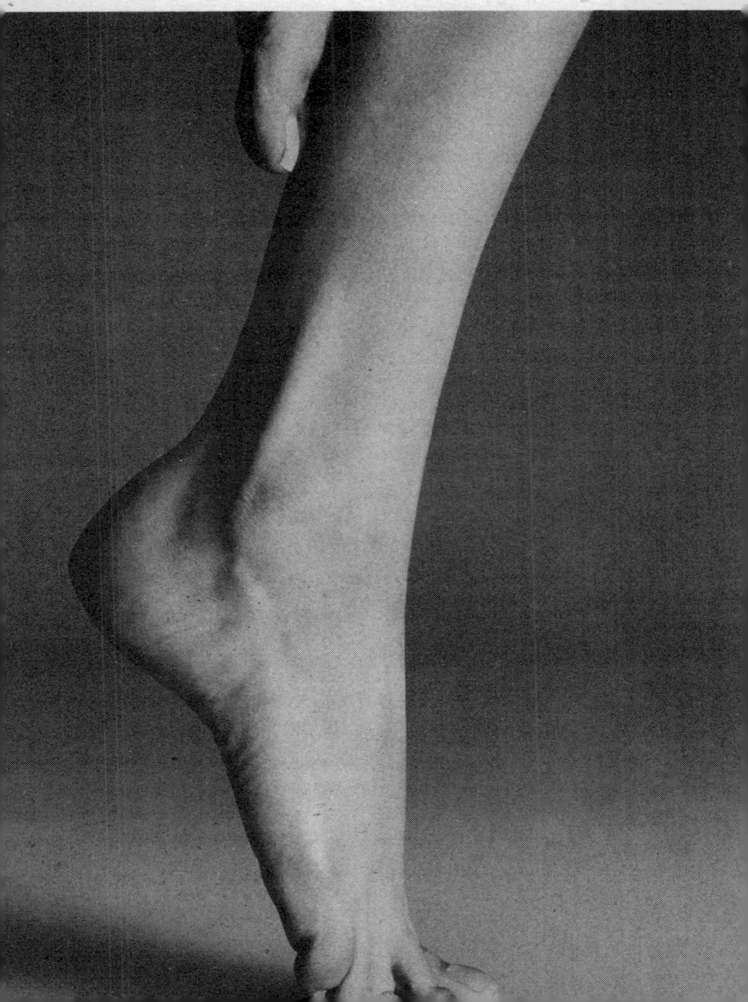

Sometimes a problem

ANKLES sometimes thicken with cellulite, for the same reasons that cellulite forms elsewhere. It is not easy to control cellulite on the ankles. The attack on the problem must always center on improving the circulation. If you can get the blood to flow back out of the ankle area, against the pull of gravity, you have a chance of solving the problem.

Lie on the floor, arms outstretched. Bring both legs
up, as illustrated, and keep them stationary. Now
point with the heels. Then point with the
toes. Feel the leg muscles stretch. Repeat 25 times.

Lying in the same position and using just
your feet, make small circles in the air, first in one
direction, then the other. Legs must remain
motionless. Repeat 15 to 25
times, in each direction.

COURTESY OF THE FRENCH GOVERNMENT TOURIST OFFICE

A few words about sports

Sports let you have fun while you keep fit. Some benefit an anti-cellulite program. Others, practiced too intensively can be detrimental.

Swimming is the only sport that anyone with cellulite can enjoy without limitation. Tennis, skiing, ice skating or bike riding should all be done in moderation—and never to exhaustion. The same applies to ballet and modern dancing. Because fatigue hinders the body from flushing out toxic materials, sports in cellulite control must never be over-tiring. Fatigue only adds to the amount of residues already present.

After cellulite has been eliminated, all sports can be considered truly desirable as a form of exercise.

Swimming is probably the perfect sport, and certainly best for anyone with a cellulite problem. It develops deeper breathing. It involves all the muscles of the body and, because the body is level, does so without pressure on any one point. When done correctly, swimming is not strenuous. It even has a strong relaxing and soothing affect on the nerves. Moreover, it stimulates circulation equally throughout the entire body. As the body glides through the water, the tissues are given a powerful hydro-massage that helps dissociate cellulite deposits while firming the skin as well. All forms of swimming are excellent, but the "crawl" is especially good for deep breathing. The "breast stroke" is an effective, natural way to exercise special problem areas—inner thighs and upper arms.

Water exercises

These all can be done by swimmers and non-swimmers alike. Work at the side of a pool—or in any other water deep enough to reach your shoulders—where you can hold on to something solid, like an anchored raft or dockside ladder. Water supports your weight so you don't feel heavy as you move. At the same time, water resists your movements, making each one more effective and beneficial.

The following four movements concentrate on firming the hip joint area and the inner thighs.

Face pool side. Feel secure as you hold the side. Raise right leg 10 times, then left leg 10 times.

Back against pool side. Hold yourself firmly as you split your legs, knees stiff. As fast as you can, bring your legs together and split again, keeping legs perfectly straight. Repeat 15 times.

Face pool side.
Place right
foot on left knee.
Swing right
knee forward and
back as far as
possible, 10 times.
Reverse legs. Swing
left knee 10 times.

Face pool side. Grasp the side securely, elbows stiff, and
spread your legs wide, as shown. Now bring your legs together
in front of you, knees stiff. Repeat 10 times.

The next exercises work on the hips, buttocks and legs.

Back against pool side. Cross your legs at the knee, keeping knees stiff. Crisscross legs rapidly 10 times. Rest. Repeat 10 times. Rest. Repeat 10 times more for a total of 30 short scissors.

Back against pool side. Bend knees
up to chest. Swing to the right,
touching knees against the side,
and then swing to the left. Repeat
10 times on each side.

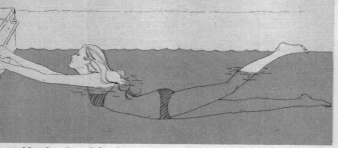

Hold side of pool firmly, arms extended as you float on your
stomach. Kick. If you keep your knees stiff, you will feel
movement all through the leg and hip area. Work as fast as
it is comfortable for you, counting to 20 or 30.

·❈9❈·

Yoga—Mind Over Matter

YOGA exercises are an excellent form of cellulite control. The various "postures" that use body weight as a resistance develop body tone. Yoga exercises every tendon, ligament and muscle of the body including those "hard-to-reach" areas seldom brought into action in other forms of movement. It improves digestion, elimination, circulation and breathing. In addition, it is a superb way to relieve tension.

Of the literally hundreds of different Yoga "postures," those presented here are simple ones especially effective in fighting cellulite. None of the more difficult exercises are suggested. If you decide you like Yoga, however, why not follow up on it? It is a form of exercise marvelously adapted to the feminine body.

Think of Yoga as the "whole body" exercise, in relation to your fight against cellulite. Although not essential to your anti-cellulite program, Yoga exercises offer the perfect way to tone and train every part of you, putting you in the best condition to experience good results from your specific area exercises. The Yoga movements suggested here require no special training but they do help you put your mind to work to control your body.

All the Yoga movements should be performed *very, very slowly*, always accompanied by proper breathing. Yoga demands particular concentration during each movement. *Under no circumstances should any movement be forced.* Far from being beneficial, forced movements can strain or harm your body. As with your regular exercises, tune into your body. Listen to it. It will tell you how far you can reach or bend. The extent to which you can bend or stretch does not matter. What *does* matter is that you give your "all" to each movement or posture.

For maximum benefits, rest a few seconds between each set of postures. Lie flat on your back and breathe deeply. While relieving the feeling of fatigue, this automatically cleanses the muscles of the toxic substances released by the contractions. It is these substances, by the way, that contribute to a feeling of fatigue.

It might be a good idea to "wake up" your body and get it headed in the right direction, by starting first with the Yoga. Choose those movements which seem to be the easiest. Do not try to test yourself or force the movements just because they appeal to you. Your body resists unaccustomed exercise. Yoga helps to prevent that soreness and stiffness. It is the relaxing way to prepare your body for the specific cellulite exercises. At the same time, it builds your "will power" to get over the first few days while you get your body ready for more intense discipline. Each day, little by little, your body will "give," and become more flexible. That is exactly what you want it to do.

To do any exercise properly, including Yoga movements, you should exhale when you bend or bring your limbs close to your body. You should inhale every time you stretch, lift or raise your body or any part of it.

You need not do every exercise suggested here. Choose those you like best and vary them from time to time. Once you have the "feel" of these movements and they become easy for you, try to do each one three times.

EASY POSTURE

Sit on a hard surface with your legs crossed, hands resting on the knees, as illustrated. Make sure your back is straight.
Breathe deep down to a count of
10 to inhale, hold for 5, and 10 to exhale.
This is the ideal way to sit down. Circulation is even.
There is no pressure on any single point of the legs as there is when sitting on a chair. What's more,
this posture is comfortable. Sit this way whenever you can, while reading, watching television, etc.

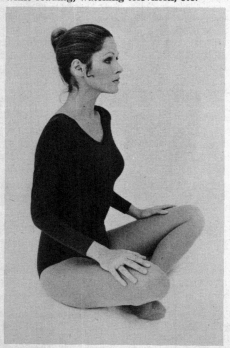

ANTI-GAS POSTURE Lying flat, *slowly* raise knees
to chest. Clasp your legs and gently press thighs against your
abdomen. You can either keep your head
on the floor or come up, as illustrated.

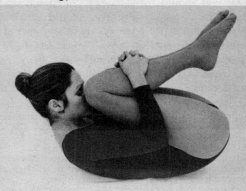

FOR INSIDE THIGH AND HIP JOINT AREA
Sit on the floor with your back straight. Keep the soles of your
feet together by clasping your hands around them.
Slowly press both knees outward toward the floor as far as you
can, without forcing, counting 1 to 5. Then
slowly bring them up. Rest and repeat.

FOR INSIDE THIGH AND HIP JOINT AREA
Clasping the soles of your feet together, while breathing out,
slowly lower your hand as far as you can comfortably.
Hold this position steadily while counting 100 to
110. Slowly come up while breathing in.

FOR INSIDE THIGH Sit with legs spread as far apart as you
can. Starting with hands on your thighs, breathe out as
you *slowly* slide them down your legs as far as you can, without
straining. When you reach your maximum position, hold it,
counting 100 to 110. Then breathe in, as you *slowly* come
back up. Rest for a few moments and repeat.

FOR THIGHS, BUTTOCKS, BACK AND ARMS Lie flat
on your stomach with your chin on the floor, arms alongside.
Bend your knees and grasp your feet with your hands. Holding your
feet firmly, raise your rib cage from the floor and tilt your head back.
Try to lift your knees off the floor. Keep this position steadily as you
count 100 to 110. Then lower your knees to the floor, still holding your
feet. Lower your trunk. Now release your feet and slowly lower them
the floor. Rest for a while with your cheek on the floor. Then repeat.

FOR HIP JOINT AREA, THIGHS AND BUTTOCKS
Sit on the floor with one leg extended in front of you. Grasp the foot
of the other leg with both hands and *slowly* lift it toward your head.
To make it easier, bend your head forward without forcing.
Instead, simply lift your leg as much as you comfortably can.
Hold the posture motionless, counting 100 to 105. Relax.
Reverse position and lift other leg.

FOR HIPS AND BUTTOCKS Lie flat on your stomach, arms alongside your body, chin resting on the floor. *Slowly* raise one leg, as illustrated. Hold steadily for the count of 10 and then *slowly* lower the leg.

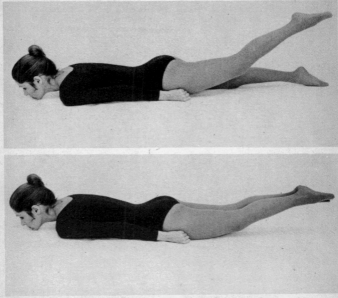

FOR BUTTOCKS Lie flat on your stomach, arms along your body, chin resting on the floor. *Slowly* lift legs off the floor while pressing down with your fists. Hold motionless for the count of 10 and then *slowly* lower the legs.

**FOR THIGHS AND
BUTTOCKS** In a standing
position, rest your hands
on your head, palms
together. Breathe out as
you *slowly* bend your knees
and lower your body until
you are resting on your
heels. Then, without stopping,
breathe in and *slowly*
raise your body
to the starting position.

FOR THIGHS AND BUTTOCKS Lying flat on
your back, arms along your body, bend your knees and rest
your feet on the floor. Then *slowly* lift buttocks off the floor and
place your hands in the small of the back, as illustrated.
Without moving, hold this posture to the
count of 10. Then *slowly* lower the body to the floor.

FOR BUTTOCKS AND THIGHS Starting from a kneeling
position, bring your right knee up in front of you.
Place right hand on right knee and left hand on left thigh. Keep
your *back straight* as you slowly push the right knee forward
as far as you can. Hold for a few seconds. Then slowly return to
starting position. Rest for awhile. Then repeat with the other leg.

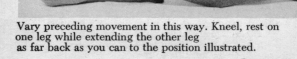

Vary preceding movement in this way. Kneel, rest on
one leg while extending the other leg
as far back as you can to the position illustrated.

FOR HIP JOINT AREA AND OUTSIDE THIGH

Sit on the floor and cross right leg over left thigh. Clasp your hands around your knees. Hold this posture motionless to the count of 10 and then *slowly* release the legs. Rest for a few seconds then repeat, crossing left leg over right thigh.

For an extra pull, bring your head toward your knee. This gives a marvelous stretch to the upper side of the thigh which is so vulnerable to cellulite.

FOR LEGS AND BUTTOCKS Lie on left side,
supporting head with your left hand. Bend right leg and grasp
the toes with your right hand. Now slowly try to straighten
the leg, as illustrated. Keep the other leg
slightly bent to maintain your balance. Hold posture for
awhile, counting 100 to 110, then change legs.

FOR LEGS, HIPS AND BUTTOCKS Lie flat on your back.
Draw knees to chest and hold your toes. *Slowly* try to straighten
your legs as close to the position illustrated as possible.
Do not force or strain. Hold whatever position you achieve
to the count of 10. Slowly release by bending knees.

FOR BACK, STOMACH AND ARMS Stand up straight,
feet slightly apart, hands along your body. Bring arms back and
clasp your hands. While breathing out, *slowly* bend down
as far as you can comfortably. Hold to the
count of 10. Then *slowly* come up while breathing in.

FOR ENTIRE BODY Kneel down, arms resting on the floor with your fingers interlocked. Place your head in your hands, letting the top of your forehead rest on the floor. Now try to straighten your legs, as illustrated. For an extra pull, slowly push yourself forward so that the torso is in a vertical position. Hold as long as you can, without strain. Then *slowly* bring the knees to the floor.

FOR BACK, STOMACH AND LEGS Sit on the floor,
legs extended, feet together. Raise your arms above your head
while inhaling. While exhaling, *slowly* bend forward as far
as you can, without forcing, and grasp your legs. Hold without
moving for awhile, at least to a count of 5. Then *slowly* come up.

FOR THE BACK Lie on the floor, face down and legs together.
Raise head and shoulders off the floor. Then place your
hands flat at shoulder level. *Very, very slowly* lift your torso up as
far as you can, without forcing. Use your arms only for support.
Do not *push* up. Hold position, counting 100 to 110. First
lower torso, then shoulders, then head, very slowly. Rest
with arms along your body, cheek on the floor.

FOR BACK, STOMACH AND LEGS Lying on back with
arms along body, *slowly* raise your legs. Lift hips off floor,
pushing with your hands against the floor. Carefully swing your
legs over your head, keeping knees straight, and touch the
floor with your toes, if possible. Be extremely careful not to force
or strain yourself in this movement. Once
you have reached your position, hold it for awhile. Then
come out of the posture *very slowly* and rest.

FOR BACK, STOMACH AND LEGS Stand up straight with feet a few inches apart. Breathe in as you bring both arms above your head. Then, as you exhale, bend down *very slowly* and grasp whatever part of your leg you can reach. Hold for awhile. Then *slowly* straighten up and rest.

SUPERB POSTURE TO FIGHT CELLULITE Lie on your back and bring knees to the chest. Then raise your hips off the floor and, holding your hands in the small of the back, slowly straighten up the legs, as shown. After holding as long as comfortable, release yourself *very slowly*. Rest and breathe deeply. In an anti-cellulite program, this posture should always be done at the end of a Yoga session. For maximum benefits, this posture should be held for 3 minutes. Start with 1 minute and gradually increase until you are able to hold it for 3 full minutes.

❈10❈

Massage—The Extra Something That Makes It Happen

Massage is a slightly forbidding word to many people. It seems to mean narcissistic, hedonistic, caring too much for your own body. It means letting someone else rub you down, knead your muscles, push, pull and pummel you. In our world, that's sometimes suspect and even taboo! It's somehow "not quite right" to let yourself relax so completely—to enjoy your body from top to toe so thoroughly. If only we could accept massage for what it really is—a perfectly healthy, positively relaxing way to tune in and tone up the body—we would find many more experienced masseurs and masseuses in every city and town! We would be in the same position as Japan, where bathing and massage are life essentials in public facilities and group activities.

But back to cellulite! Cellulite massage uses the movements and techniques of regular body massage adapted to the specific requirements of each area and to the structure of the lumps and bumps themselves. *You massage yourself!* There's nothing hedonistic or luxurious about this at all. Rather, it is a very *businesslike* method of loosening your lumps!

Perhaps businesslike is a grim word. You already know that your cellulite program isn't all penance and discipline. You can eat many foods you like which are even good for you! You can exercise in a number of unique, relaxing ways to attack those bulges, and feel great as a result. The breathing and elimination suggestions help you to function more smoothly—give you more energy, better sleep and more relaxed attitudes. The cellulite plan is a very positive approach to a problem with lots of fringe benefits.

Think of it positively. And let's talk about massage as an integral part of your plan.

Cellulite masage *is* businesslike because it treats the problem where it lies. *You* rub, stroke, knead, knuckle, wring the lumps, bumps and bulges where they exist. The effect is both physical and mental. Physically you can feel those lumps, those pockets of trapped fat. You can even work out some of your frustrations! You hit, you pound, you attack the causes of your anger and despair. You can spank them like naughty children. You can wring them out of your system, literally as well as figuratively. Mentally, just because you can do something positive, active and quite physical about cellulite, your mind seems to lighten as you work to loosen the cellulite. You are in actual touch with what is causing you much distress—with what is bothering you and what, up to now, has been a hopeless problem.

The massage part of your program should be considered the most personal, most intimate and, in some ways, the most direct of all suggested methods of cellulite control.

Massage has a track record

Massage has been practiced for thousands of years. Even primitive peoples, acting almost solely through instinct, used it as a therapeutic remedy. Chinese documents, written as early as 3,000 B.C., praise the effects of rhythmically rubbing and kneading the body. Ancient Hindu doctors highly recommended the technique. And it was a favorite of the early Egyptians. The Greek physician, Hippocrates, the father of modern medicine, was a great advocate of the value of massage combined with correct diet, fresh air and exercise. Massage has marvelous credentials.

Cellulite massage

We can thank the original team of Swedish masseurs and doctors who discovered cellulite for perfecting the special massage techniques that break down lumpy, cellulite nodes. It dissolves them directly and, by increasing circulation, it stimulates a freer flow of body fluids. As you already know, cellulite is a build-up of fat, body fluids and toxic residues trapped in the tissues. In order to release these trapped substances, the vessels that carry lymph and other cleansing fluids must be unclogged so that the waste materials can be flushed out.

Exercise, as we have already discussed, is invaluable in your anti-cellulite plan. Now you know why and how. Specific cellulite massage works in conjunction with exercise. It is a means of speeding up the process of dissolving bulges. Two particularly responsive areas are the inside of the knee and the upper thigh. The upper thigh is made up mainly of ligaments that surround the hip joint. On so many women, these ligaments are topped by a layer of hardened fat and dense cellulite. These are the "riding breeches" that ruin so many figures. Massage, combined with exercise, can really make the difference here. The buttocks, tummy and hips also respond beautifully to the cellulite massage. Let's learn the techniques that result in a quicker, more thorough elimination of cellulite.

How should you massage?

At first, *go easy*. Stroke, knead, rub, etc., with moderate, firm, not-too-heavy pressure, *taking care not to press hard enough to bruise yourself or break any capillaries*. Besides, if you press too firmly, you will irritate your nervous system. Since cellulite areas are already sensitive in many cases, you'll know easily enough if you are applying too much pressure. As your tissues become more supple, you'll be able to massage more vigorously.

How long should you massage?

Depending upon the thickness of the cellulite, work 10 to 20 minutes on a particular area. Ten minutes should be sufficient for the tummy but don't hesitate to devote up to 20 minutes to the upper thighs and hips.

When should you massage?

Massage can be included in your daily schedule without a lot of nuisance. Like any other therapeutic method, massage must be regular to be effective. If you can't manage it every day try for at least every other day.

There are a few simple ways to incorporate self-massage into your life. The easiest is to massage in the tub. The sitting position is very good for working on the legs and upper arms. You can work on the buttocks and hips after you towel dry. If you prefer a shower, be sure you are secure and steady on your feet. Use a rubber bath mat or those non-slip strips for safety in the tub.

You can quietly massage while watching television or driving on long trips—when someone else is at the wheel. You don't need lots of space or any special clothes. You just need a strong desire to get rid of your cellulite.

You can massage any time of the day but it's best to wait at least two hours after eating. The most convenient time for most women is after the bath or shower—and preferably one that includes a brisk body rub with a loofah friction mitt. A bath is relaxing and massage benefits you most when you are relaxed. You are better off skipping the massage if you are tense or in a rush. When you are tense, or hurried, you constrict the channels through which the released wastes and residues from the massage are flushed out.

What are the massage movements used?

There are five massage movements used to help break down cellulite. They are: stroking, kneading, knuckling, "S" formation and wringing. Each has a specific value in the prescribed order and performs a different function.

Light stroking prepares the skin for the massage movements that will follow. Wringing, knuckling and "S" formation, all forms of kneading, break down and dissolve the cellulite nodes. It is the deep stroking, always used at the end of each session, that helps send the wastes loosened by kneading on their way through the system and out of the body. *If the deep stroking is omitted or neglected, the value of the entire massage is lost.* So, by all means, follow the specific progression as it is listed.

Light Stroking describes the long, fluid movements that "caress" the skin in one direction only—toward the heart. This massage step readies the area for the heavier movements that follow.

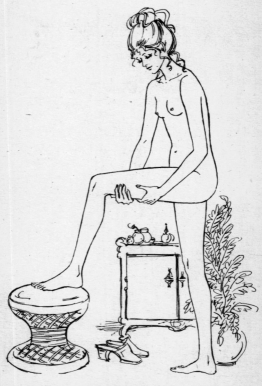

Place your hands flat and gently curve your fingers to conform to the shape of the area being massaged. With a sliding movement, stroke the area, always going upward toward the heart when doing legs and hips and clockwise when doing the tummy.

Kneading is grasping a "hunk" of flesh, lifting it away from the underlying structure and squeezing it. You can do this with your fingers or with your whole hand.

In *Finger Kneading* thumb and fingertips lift the
skin from the underlying tissues and squeeze it. Lift and
squeeze, lift and squeeze. You may find it easier to work
standing up, with your leg resting on a stool, tub side, etc.,
but you can relax and sit down too. Pinching brings the
blood closer to the surface and helps dissipate wastes.
Fingers can work all over but they fit most easily into the
smaller areas like the inner knee, the upper arm and
the ankle.

In *Hand Kneading* you lift and squeeze with the whole hand. This works well on larger areas where you can really grasp a large piece of flesh.

Here the movement is just like kneading dough or squeezing out a sponge. Use one or two hands depending on the size of the area. As you can see, you can work with one hand on each buttock (fig. 1), one hand on either side of the leg (fig. 2) or with both hands on the same side of the leg. (fig. 3)

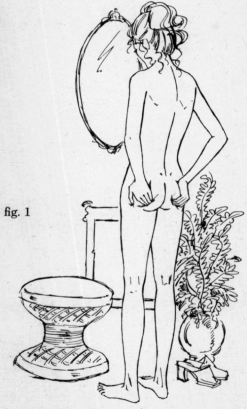

fig. 1

The standing position is important when working from upper thighs to upper hips. When you massage any part of the leg below the upper thigh, rest that leg on a stool, tub side or the like to relax your muscles.

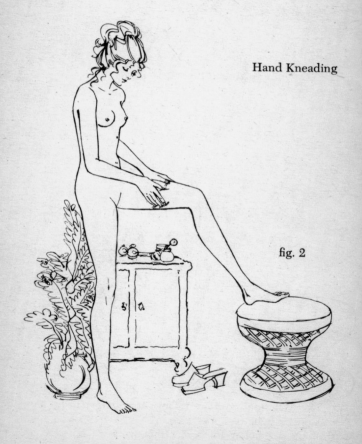

Hand Kneading

fig. 2

fig. 3

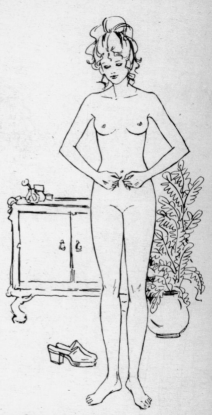

Knuckling is a crushing movement done in a circular direction with fingers curled so that the knuckles press the skin. Here's where you can really dig in, crush cellulite, beat it to a pulp and battle those bulges. If your cellulite is the firm or solid variety, this step should follow *Light Stroking*. You will not be able to lift and squeeze solid cellulite. Knuckling is excellent for hips, upper thighs and tummy.

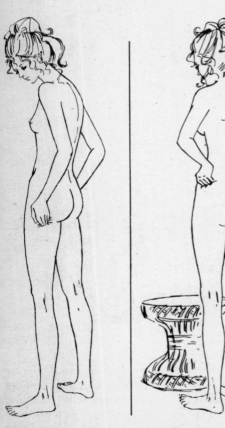
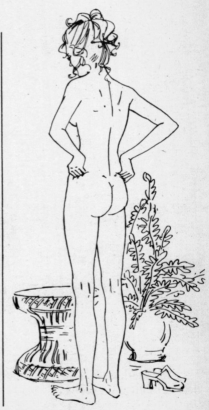

"S" *Formation* uses the thumb and fingers of both hands to lift up a portion of flesh. The hands go back and forth in opposite directions to form an "S" shape fold.

Move those mounds around. Don't let them just sit there. This is deep massage and you will feel some action. Work slowly and steadily for best results. Lift and twist on the tummy, hips, thighs and around the knee, inside and out.

Wringing is basically the "S" Formation done without picking up the flesh. This is deep action massage. Once again, you can really get down to the cellulite, grit your teeth and wring it out of your life!

Rest both hands around the area and twist back and forward. This should remind you of wringing clothes. This offers an alternative to the "S" Formation for those with solid cellulite. Wringing should be done in any position where your leg muscles are completely relaxed, leg raised or sitting down. The large area of the thigh is highly receptive to wringing massage.

Deep Stroking ends every massage. It is a heavy stroking movement, at full pressure, going in the direction of the heart. This increases blood and lymph circulation, relieves congestion and speeds removal of waste matter from the tissues. As in *Light Stroking*, use the whole hand, placed flat, fingers curved. With a sliding movement, exert pressure while you stroke toward the heart, up on legs and hips, clockwise on tummy. This drains the waste products released by the other massage manipulations.

When you get to *Deep Stroking*, try doing the movements while applying some scented body lotion. This will make it possible to use heavy pressure firmly and evenly in one long smooth stroke. And you will end your massage with a feeling of well-being as well as accomplishment!

Sea water massage

The rich waters of the ocean create a natural massage *milieu* that provides one of the most pleasant ways to get a body rub. Sea algae has long been associated with an ability to help speed up the destruction of cellulite lumps. Directed at the body in the strength of a wave, sea water becomes an incomparable, natural masseur. Enjoy nature's massage whenever you are near the surf:

Position yourself in the water so that the waves break against your cellulite areas.

Lie down at the water's edge and let the waves slap against you.

Walk along the water's edge, just where the waves are breaking. This is quite soothing for legs that tire easily and is particularly good for the ankles.

A terrific massage right in your own backyard

Using a garden spray hose, open the faucet full strength. Starting at the ankle, direct the hose at an angle, as illustrated, and work up to the hips. Do both legs all around—front, sides and back. Then concentrate on the problem spots, always working upward. Finish by spraying the whole leg, from the bottom up, once again. You'll need about 10 to 20 minutes.

This hydro-massage stimulates circulation, helps break down cellulite deposits and tones the tissues.

❧11❧

Relax And Let Go

Your body, human and frail though it may seem, is still the most marvelous feat of engineering, more complex than an intricate precision instrument. Everything must be in balance for the "instrument" to work properly. When your body is functioning smoothly, at its best, it is in "good health." In good health, your body can easily dispose of the ordinary toxic wastes it temporarily houses during the course of day-to-day living. When you are fatigued or tense, however, your body is less able to throw off these wastes. The result is often cellulite and the process, unfortunately, is cyclical. The more toxic wastes in your body, the more hypertensive you become. The more nervous you become the more cellulite you are likely to accumulate.

A certain amount of fatigue is normal, even desirable. It is actually a warning given by the body when physical or mental activity becomes too taxing. For this kind of fatigue, sleep is the natural antidote. The dangerous fatigue is the kind we see so much of these days— constantly tired people, lethargic people, nervous people. Tension is to blame.

Both men and women are subject to the hectic, demanding pace of modern-day living, probably the greatest cause of tension. As a woman, though, you are more prone to fatigue because your system has to grapple with a cyclical flow of hormones that are regularly altering your body's chemical balance.

The woman who works has to worry about catching her bus on time, being packed in a subway train, gulping down a sandwich at noontime so she can squeeze in a few minutes for shopping. This is not to mention the tasks that await her when she gets home! The housewife, too, is subject to much tension. What could be more mentally fatiguing than trying to bring up children, keeping track of the family's complex schedule and attempting to make ends meet on a limited budget? In addition to many irritants, both groups of women are subject to a constant barrage of noise—a particularly potent cause of tension.

Tension can also develop as a result of boredom with a job or life situation; inability to adapt to one's environment; various emotions like anger or fear; mental states like frustration, dissatisfaction and worry; and the thousand and one little problems of daily life.

Learning how to relax is very important in cellulite control

Because stress and tension are such predictable causes of cellulite, it's important to learn how to really "let go"— to totally relax your mind *and* body. Time devoted to relaxation is especially important after every exercise session. And it's paramount to make relaxation a way of life because it equalizes circulation, works to loosen up overtaxed muscles and facilitates release of toxic substances.

Knowing how to relax is a must. Some of the most common advice heard nowadays is "slow down," "relax," or "take it easy." This advice is easier to give than to follow. The truth is that the art of relaxation must be learned. Wanting to be calm is not enough. As a matter of fact, trying to force yourself may actually result in increased tension. The more you try, the more anxious you become, and so on.

The best way to relax your mind is through your body. Studies done in various countries have proved this to be true. Reduce the physical symptoms of anxiety and the anxiety will become milder. Loosening stiff muscles helps to dispel the feeling of emotional stiffness. A very popular expression is "up tight"—and with good reason. When you are emotionally tense, you do feel tight. Your heart beats faster. Your diaphragm contracts and hinders normal breathing. The flow of blood to your arms and legs is reduced. (You must have had the sensation of cold hands and feet in a tense situation at one time or another.) A number of muscles, particularly those in the arms and legs and at the nape of the neck stiffen. So does the spinal cord.

Relaxing after a day's work lets you recoup your physical and nervous strength. It also soothes you if you haven't had a good night's rest or have been engaged in particularly strenuous activity.

How is anxiety manifested physically?

When you are confronted with a situation which weighs you down emotionally, breathing becomes difficult. In a really tense situation, you may even gasp for air. This is because emotions block the diaphragm, the very powerful muscle that separates the lungs and heart from the abdominal cavity. That feeling of a knot in your stomach comes from the tightening of the diaphragm.

Anxiety and tension are apparent with nervous people who often do everything too fast—eating, talking, walking and even thinking. This is where the expression "nervous energy" comes from.

Nervous fatigue, frustration and anxiety also provoke muscular contraction in other parts of the body, particularly the neck, limbs and back. This can be terribly painful and terribly depressing as well.

The first thing is to slow down. Actions will become less jerky, thinking will become deeper and more rational. Energy not expended needlessly can be called on for situations in which it is really needed. This involves the following:

1— Gaining respiratory control in order to breathe smoothly and evenly.

2— Loosening the diaphragm by doing special exercises.

3— Learning how to voluntarily decontract muscles.

4— Improving circulation.

Learning how to relax requires good discipline and regular practice. There are many different techniques. Here are two of the most classic. Try them both and see which suits you best. They are equally good and can be done easily enough by anyone.

Description of total relaxation

1. By using your head alone, as your body is stretched out, you can easily relax.

   Lie flat on your back, preferably on a hard surface such as a carpeted floor or exercise mat. Close your eyes. Place your arms straight along your body, with hands falling naturally in a half-open position (palms facing up or down, depending upon what is natural to you). Keep legs apart with toes pointing outward.

   Now, concentrate on your toes by thinking just about them and trying to feel them, yet without moving them. Tell your toes to become limp. Order them to relax. Do this for a few seconds.

   Next, concentrate on your feet to the exclusion of all other parts of you body. Order them to become limp and relax. Now do the same thing with your ankles and work up the entire body by concentrating on one part at a time: legs, knees, thighs, abdomen, buttocks, back, chest, hands, arms, shoulders, neck and finally the face—mouth, eyes, forehead. Every part should be completely relaxed and free of tension. Your entire body will feel limp and quite heavy.

   Now you must clear your mind—reduce your thoughts to an absolute minimum, especially those that cause tension. Try to substitute a pleasant thought, such as a beautiful blue sky, a clear mountain lake. Breathe deeply and slowly. After a few minutes, you will be completely and blissfully relaxed.

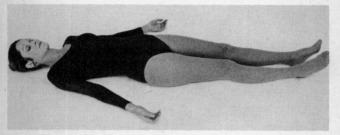

2. By using your head and body together, you have another way to relax.

The *second relaxation* exercise is similar to the first. But instead of just thinking about each area of the body, you actually contract or tighten that area, holding it for a moment before letting go. This produces the limp, heavy feeling that leads to total relaxation. Again, work on each area of your body from the toes up.

You will probably have to practice for a few weeks before you will be able to reach a state of relaxation rapidly. In the beginning, it will take from 10 to 25 minutes to relax. As you train yourself, however, it will come quite quickly—almost instantly.

Once you have mastered the technique you will be able to use it anywhere, even sitting down in a taxi, for example, or at your office. You can use it *any time* you feel tense or nervous, to calm down and regain complete control of yourself.

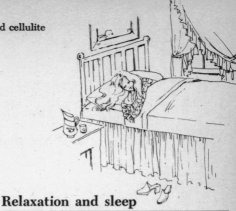

Relaxation and sleep

When you are tired, your inclination is to sleep. You need sleep to "recharge your batteries," regain your strength, maintain your equilibrium. Without sleep, you cannot go on for very long. Although science does have some knowledge of sleep, the investigation of this bodily state is still in its infancy. It is known, however, that during sleep most of the body's activities are reduced to their lowest levels. The heart beats more slowly, blood pressure drops, respiration becomes slower and more irregular. Metabolism is at its lowest rate principally because muscle activity is also at its lowest level. Body temperature falls but sweat secretion is increased considerably. Tear and salivary secretions, on the other hand, are decreased. The secretion of gastric juices does not change much and contractions and digestion continue normally.

Science aside, we all know what happens when we don't get the necessary sleep. Body and mind are simply unable to function at their maximum capacity. Unfortunately, insomnia is all too common in our hectic times. Being excited or overly anxious makes you unable to fall asleep, or unable to sleep restfully if you manage to doze off. The sleep that follows relaxation of both body and mind is deeper, far more refreshing and satisfying than ordinary sleep. It is rare when someone whose nervous system is strained or over-tired experiences normal, refreshing sleep. More often than not, this sleep is fitful and restless. You awaken tired and fatigued rather than rejuvenated. Anxiety, insomnia and fatigue form a classic trio.

Nature's tricks to promote good sleep

Nutritional factors known to contribute to sound sleep are calcium and Vitamins B and D. Some of the B vitamins which have a soothing effect on the nervous system, can be found in wheat germ, brewers' yeast, liver and molasses. Dark molasses, milk and yogurt are all good sources of both calcium and Vitamin D.

A glass of fortified warm milk containing two teaspoons of dark molasses is an excellent sedative drink to take before bedtime. You can prepare fortified milk by adding one or two tablespoonfuls of powdered skim milk to a glass of fresh milk. If you are particularly tense, take two calcium tablets with the warm milk and molasses.

A cup of warm linden blossom tea is delicious just before retiring, and is an age-old sleep-inducing *tisane*. If you like, you can add a teaspoon of honey to sweeten it.

Right before going to sleep, take a dozen *Complete Breaths* in front of an open window.

Always be sure your room remains well-ventilated.

Baths and relaxation

A bath is very relaxing. It relieves tension, calms the nerves and is a marvelous preparation for a good night's sleep.

Take advantage of your bath, making it a real beauty treat, not just a way to get clean. Give yourself as much time as possible. Enjoy it. Practice the *Total Relaxation* exercise. Feel the sensuous pleasure, the delight of water caressing every inch of your skin. Try one of the small rubber head pillows designed for use in the tub, so you can be completely at ease. And always remember that *baths should be warm, not hot*. Hot water tends to dry the skin, making it saggy in due time.

Here are a number of special baths you might try for their beautifying and relaxing effects:

Oil Bath: If your skin is dry, this is the bath for you. It will give you a feeling of pure luxury as it moisturizes dry skin. Try one of the many fragrant bath oils on the market or make one of your own: Pour eight ounces of any pure vegetable oil—corn, peanut or olive oil—into a bottle or jar. Combine in a cup three ounces of water and one-half ounce of a mild detergent shampoo. Add some of your favorite perfume and funnel or pour the mixture into the oil. Cap the jar or bottle and shake it well to blend all ingredients. Add a few ounces to a warm bath, shaking the jar before each use. This provides a superb, personalized bath oil for just pennies!

As a variation, substitute a few drops of essential oil for your favorite perfume. Essential oils are pure aromatic extract of fruit or flowers. They are increasingly popular as a way to create your own personal fragrance.

Herbal Bath: This is soothing for irritated nerves. Put a tablespoonful or two of mint, eucalyptus leaves or pine needles into a piece of cheesecloth and tie up the ends. Add this aromatic bag to a warm bath. If you prefer, you can use any fresh herb from your garden. You can also prepare an herb bath by putting two heaping tablespoonfuls of any of the above mentioned herbs, or a combination of rosemary and peppermint, into a pint of water. Bring this to boil and simmer for two minutes. After straining, mix the hot infusion with a pint of cider vinegar. Let this stand for 48 hours before using. Add one cup to a warm bath. All these herbal baths are delightfully relaxing.

Mineral Bath: This bath is especially stimulating and toning, and it works wonders for tension and fatigue! While the water is running, add 1½ cups of Epsom salts to the bath. Soak in the tub for at least 20 minutes. You'll emerge quite tranquil and refreshed.

*The following three baths are particularly
beneficial for cellulite control:*

Salt Bath: This reducing and purifying bath is the exception to the "hot-tub" rule. Put two pounds of coarse kitchen salt into a hot tub and soak yourself for 30 minutes. Then shower briefly with warm water. Now wrap up in a large towel and quickly pat dry without rubbing. Lie down under a few heavy blankets and you will perspire abundantly, helping your system to cleanse itself of cellulite-causing impurities.

Sea Bath at Home: You can actually take a sea bath at home by dissolving several handfuls of natural sea salt in a tub of warm water and relaxing for 20 minutes. This salt has a high concentration of sea minerals, good for reducing tension and fatigue as they work toward breaking down cellulite.

Seaweed Bath: Seaweed, because of its iodine content, is exceptionally good in combatting cellulite. Simply put fresh or dried seaweed, tied loosely in a piece of cheese cloth, into a warm tub. (If you like, you can add some pine needles to give the bath a pleasant aroma.) While in the tub, squeeze the seaweed bag the way you would a sponge, to release its beneficial properties, and rub it on your cellulite lumps. Soak as long as you like—the longer the better!

Because a bath is so relaxing, it's best to shower rather than bathe in the morning. A shower followed by a brisk toweling and friction rub is quite invigorating and awakening. If you feel you must bathe in the morning, make it a very brief bath and stand under a cool shower afterwards. Or try your bath-this way: Let half the warm water run out of the tub and run the cool water full force. Lie back and feel your whole body tingle! You'll find this most stimulating and refreshing, and not cold at all. Follow with a brisk toweling and friction rub.

How does a slant board help you relax?

When you lie down in a slanting position, feet higher than your head, you reverse the pull of gravity of the body fluids. This calms you down, soothes your nerves and is superb for improving circulation—all necessary in the fight against cellulite. Although there are many slant boards on the market, you can easily make your own with a board about 6 feet long and 18 inches wide. Raise one end 15 inches from the floor, and cover it with a blanket. Lie on your slant board, feet elevated, with your hands along your body and eyes closed for 15 minutes before sleeping. Combine this with the *Total Relaxation* exercise. It's wonderful after a full day's work and a splendid way to prepare for good sleep.

Aside from the work it does in cellulite control, a slant board will do wonders for your complexion and hair by rushing an extra supply of blood to your head thus providing additional nourishment to face and scalp.

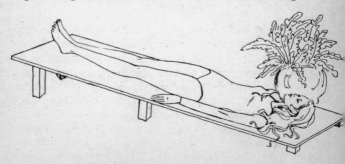

Epilogue

Putting it all together

I have set down the correct methods in every phase of cellulite control. So now you have all the information you need to fight your cellulite problem. You can use it in any way that best fits your life.

To get the most from the program, *you must really want to solve your problem.* It's best to work out a personal schedule that allows you maximum time for exercise and massage. The first few weeks you will have to spend more time on yourself to develop a schedule rhythm, to find the right time to do what you have to do—shop for and prepare the meals, practice deep breathing, do your special cellulite exercise and massage. There are several alternatives in the program. This is to accommodate the different life styles of different women. With practice, you'll learn to do your cellulite routine in no time!

I have written this book in response to the voluminous mail I receive every month that I cannot possibly answer individually. I've shown you what causes cellulite and what to do about it. Read carefully. Think positively. Work slowly but surely. You *can* control cellulite. But it's up to *you.*

Bonne chance,

Nicole Ronsard

Nicole Ronsard

About the Author

Nicole Ronsard is one of the world's foremost authorities on cellulite, a physical condition that has plagued women everywhere. Although cellulite is well known throughout Europe, when Mme. Ronsard came to the United States, she found that Americans had scarcely heard of the condition.

A graduate of the Ecole Supérieure de Paris in Esthétique Corporelle (science related to body shaping techniques), Mme. Ronsard spent several years researching the most advanced therapies for cellulite control in European centers. She has incorporated her years of experience into a successful method of slenderizing which has gained for her an indisputable reputation in her field.

For seven years, 1967 through 1974, Mme. Ronsard operated her internationally renowned Salon in New York City, the first of its kind in the United States devoted exclusively to the treatment of cellulite. Her book is the direct result of the successful treatment given at her Salon and makes it possible for women everywhere to control this condition.

The book was an immediate success and became a national bestseller. Mme. Ronsard carried the cellulite message throughout the country on television, radio, in newspapers and lectures.

In response to the many inquiries of concerned women, Mme. Ronsard recently developed the MULTI-TONER, an exercise aid specifically designed to firm up inner thighs and upper arms, two chronic trouble spots with women of all ages.

Mme. Ronsard has completed her second book, "NICOLE RONSARD'S NO-EXCUSE EXERCISE GUIDE" and is currently working on a third book which will concern itself with the many directions cellulite awareness can take.

Mme. Ronsard is married to Marcel Ronsard, a business executive. The Ronsards live in New York City with their son Eric.

_____ Notes_____